Sports Law in China

Sports Law in China

Second Edition

Junxin Kang
Jing Xia
Chun Shen
Shuiqing Liu
Yang Chen
Feng Wu

This book was originally published as a monograph in the International Encyclopaedia of Laws/Sports Law.

Founding Editor: Roger Blanpain
General Editor: Frank Hendrickx
Volume Editor: Michele Colucci

Wolters Kluwer

Published by:
Kluwer Law International B.V.
PO Box 316
2400 AH Alphen aan den Rijn
The Netherlands
Website: www.wolterskluwerlr.com

Sold and distributed in North, Central and South America by:
Wolters Kluwer Legal & Regulatory U.S.
7201 McKinney Circle
Frederick, MD 21704
United States of America
Email: customer.service@wolterskluwer.com

Sold and distributed in all other countries by:
Quadrant
Rockwood House
Haywards Heath
West Sussex
RH16 3DH
United Kingdom
Email: international-customerservice@wolterskluwer.com

Printed on acid-free paper

ISBN 97890-411-8756-7

e-Book: ISBN 97890-411-8779-6
web-PDF: ISBN 97890-411-8809-0

This title is available on www.kluwerlawonline.com

Printed and Bound by CPI Group (UK) Ltd, Croydon, CR0 4YY.

The Authors

Prof. Junxinkang (1968–), a Chinese famous jurist, graduated from Wuhan University in 1996, Ph.D. Now, he is a professor of both Wuhan University and Zhongnan University of Economics and Law. He also served as the Vice President of China Society of Criminology, and the Chairman of Criminal Law Research Association of Hubei Province Law Society. He was a visiting scholar of Southern Illinois University Law school in the US in 2010.

Prof. Kang's teaching and research covers Criminal Law, Criminology, Sports Law and other fields, and has a fruitful research results. His research achievement mainly includes three individual monographs which consisted of "Principles of Criminal Law of Life" in 2009, "Ideal and the Reality—China's Death Penalty System Report" in 2005, and "Court Reform" in 2004. He is also the chief editor of fifteen books, and the co-author of twenty works. He also had published more than hundred academic papers in Chinese core journals.

Professor Kang is also devoted to the study of the sports law. He is the one of the first batch of China's Sports Law Ph.D. tutor, one of the Ten Young Jurists in Hubei Province, who has quite accomplished in the anti-doping and sports conflict research. In recent years, he has a very good research results, which mainly includes *the Research of the Guilty Person in Competitive Sports* (2009), *The Outline of the Research of the Sports Crime* (2009), *Conviction of Doping Issues* (2010), *Summary of Sports Crimes in China* (2010), *Bribery in Professional Football League in China* (2012), *The Study of Injury Behavior in Competitive Sports* (2012), *Legal Analysis of Fair Charles in Sports* (2013), *Legal Regulation of Gender Discrimination in Sport* (2013), *Antitrust Examination of Marketing Rights in Sports Broadcasting* (2014) and so on. He also received the subject of the focus of the research institute in Hubei of strategy of development of the rule of law in 2013: *Proposed Draft of Experts Modification of "LAW OF THE PEOPLE'S REPUBLIC OF CHINA ON PHYSICAL CULTURE AND SPORT"*.

In recent years, he has chaired more than ten national and ministerial projects, including the National Social Science Fund, National Research Projects of the Rule of Law and

The Authors

Legal Theory of the Ministry of Justice, Sport Philosophy and Social Science Research Projects of General Administration of Sports of China (GASC), the projects of European Commission on Human Rights, the projects of the British Foreign Office, etc.
Prof. Kang's has won so many honors from his works and projects, mainly the Outstanding Achievement Award of Twelfth Chinese Book, the Award for excellence research of Chinese Research Society of Criminology in decade, the first prize of the First Rule Forum of Central China, first prize of the First Rule Forum of Hubei Province.

Dr. Jing Xia (1981–), associate professor of Jianghan University, obtained bachelor degree in Law (specialization in International Economic Law) in 2004, master degree in Sports Law Education (specialization in Sports Law) in 2008 and has obtained Ph.D. degree in Law in 2011. Her main research domain covers private international law, criminal law and sports law. She has published sixteen papers related to Sports Law. She supervised two projects: one is doctoral student team project of Wuhan University, the other is project of China Postdoctoral Science Foundation and has participated six sports-related projects in national level.

Dr. Feng Wu (1982–), lawyer of Hongtop Ansion Law Firm. She graduated from Wuhan University in 2013, Ph.D. Her main research area includes sports law, criminal law and criminology. Dr. Wu likes broadly participating in some academic subject projects, so she has published more than ten academic articles. Some of her articles, *On the Issues about the Crime of Refusing to Pay Remuneration in Criminal Law*

Amendment (Eighth) and *On Perfecting the Legislation of Future Crimes in China* have got high evaluation. In addition, she is a lawyer, which helps her can dedicate to direct legal theory and practice issues in long term.

Chun Shen (1982–), is a teacher of Changsha University of Science and Technology, who obtained Ph.D. degree from Wuhan University in 2014. He also served as the assistant dean of Law Department of Changsha University of Science and Technology. Dr. Shen had been to Liberia and worked as a teacher in Liberia University which is the famous university in West Africa. His teaching and research areas include Sports Law and Criminal Law. He has already published a number of academic papers, including *The Six Conception Transitions In The Eighth Criminal Law Amendment.*

Shuiqing Liu (1981–), a Chinese young jurist, graduated from Wuhan University in 2015, Ph.D. Now, he is working as a lecturer of physical culture institute of Henan Normal University. He obtained his bachelor's degree in Education in 2006, Master Degree in Sport Education in 2009. He had worked as a teacher of Tongren Polytechnic in Guizhou province for three years. His main research domain covers sports law and sports crimes. He has published eleven papers related to sports law, including *Legal Regulation of Gender Discrimination in Sport* (2013), and *Countermeasures of EU for Violence of Football Audience* (2014) and so on.

The Authors

Yang Chen (1987–) is a student of Wuhan University and is pursuing Doctorate in Sports Law. His main research domain includes sports law, criminal law and criminology. In the filed of sports law, he is focused on research of field security, including spectator violence, collective behaviors and anti terrorism in sports field, etc. In addition, he is keen on practical work, especially in public welfare, He has worked at the legal aid center of Wuhan University for a year.

Table of Contents

Table of Contents

Table of Contents

Table of Contents

List of Abbreviations

CAD	Civil Affairs Department
CAS	Court of Arbitration for Sport
CHINADA	China Anti-Doping Agency
COC	Chinese Olympic Committee
GASC	General Administration of Sports of China
IOC	International Olympic Committee
NPC	The National People's Congress
NPCC	National Paralympic Committee of China
NSCC	Beijing National Sport Century Sporting Goods Quality Certification Centre
PRC	The People's Republic of China
SAD	Sports Administrative Department
SCNPC	Standing Committee of the National People's Congress
TUE	Therapeutic Use Exemption
VAT	Value Added Tax
WADA	World Anti-Doping Agency
WADC	World Anti-Doping Code

Preface

In 2012, Sports Law in China (1st Edition) has been published by Kluwer Law International in the Netherlands. In the past four years, the physical culture of China has undergone a dramatic transformation and has made enormous achievements. At the same time, this book, which introduces Chinese sports law to the whole world, has also been recognized and praised by academia. What is more, it won the highest award of the 13th Outstanding Achievement Award in the Humanities and Social Sciences Research of Wuhan University.

China's sports law is constantly moving forward; we need to update the book to let it move with the times. So I organized a team to complete the work of writing timely when I had been invitated by Prof. Dr. Frank Hendrickx on the publication of Sport Law in China (2nd Edition). In the past year and a half, although we had encountered a number of difficulties including the restructuring of the research system, the adjustment of whole book structure and the exchange of writers and other issues, our team was able to overcome the difficulties and completed the writing in the end.

On behalf of my team, I would like to thank Kluwer Law International Press. They provide a nice communication and cooperation platform for international sports legal system.

We would like to thank Prof. Dr. Frank Hendrickx, General Editor of the International Encyclopaedia of Laws as well as Mr. Joeri Lauwers, assistant publisher at Kluwer Law International. Without their professional dedication and hard work neither this book nor the cooperation would have been possible.

Furthermore, we would like to thank Dr. Yong Zhu, associate professor of Zhongnan University of Economics and Law who helped us in the English proofreading.

Finally, we would like to extend our thanks to General Administration of Sport of China and Wuhan University for their concern and support.

Wuhan University
June 27, 2016
Junxin Kang

General Introduction

Chapter 1. General Background

§1. The Origin of Sports in China

1. Chinese sports culture enjoys a long history, which dates back to prehistoric time. During this time period, sports were in primitive forms and were played in different forms in every historical phase. They have evolved over a series of such historical periods from Xia Shang and Zhou dynasties to Ming and Qing dynasties and so on.

Sports originated in China mainly for the following reasons: survival and production needs; primitive religious ritual needs; original entertainment needs; military security needs; health care needs.

§2. The Origin of Sports Law in China

2. The evolvement of the sports law in China is divided into three stages as follows.

I. Customs Stage

3. Customs were the initial forms and indispensable stages of law. During this period, low levels of productivity made sports activities small and irregular, so the activities were regulated by the customs. Different sports developed various customs which in turn regulated the sports activities.

II. Rules Stage

4. With the continuous development of society, the scale of sports became larger and the forms of sports became much more. People spent more time and energy on the sports, which generated sports professionals. During that time, sports became independent of the society and the corresponding rules also came out. For example, the rules of playing Cu Ju (the ancient form of football in China).

Cu Ju, the original form of football, is a kind of skill and sports prevailed among people, even army officers, in ancient China which had an influence on other nationalities and became widespread gradually all over the world as an important culture of China Han nationality. It was entered in the First List of National Intangible Cultural Heritage with approval of China State Council on May 20, 2006.[1]

III. Law Stage

5. With the continuous development of Chinese sports, Chinese sports law was produced. From the customs stage and rules stage to the law stage, it had experienced a series of complex processes. With the high level of social development, the existence of law is necessary. Therefore, the generation of Chinese sports law is historically inevitable. From the Qing government to the present, China has enacted a series of sports laws. These laws are effective in regulating and promoting the development of sports. Today, the current main law in sports is "Law of the People's Republic China on Physical Culture and Sports".

1. Picture source: http://baike.baidu.com/view/17514.htm?fr=aladdin.

Chapter 2. Development of Sports Law

§1. The Development of Sports Law of Qing Government

I. Overall Situation of Sports Law of Qing Government

6. In the late Qing dynasty, the government began to learn Western legal systems and reform the China's legal system. Although no specific legislation on sports was adopted, relevant stipulation appeared in some regulations. Regulations related to sports in late Qing dynasty were as follows.[2]

A. Imperial Schools' Charter

7. In 1902, the Qing government promulgated the "Imperial Schools' Charter," which was also called "Renyin school system." This charter was drawn up by Mr. Zhang Baixi, and approved by the Qing government. This Charter divided the school into seven levels; schools under the higher ones were required to learn gymnastics. However, it was abolished before its implementation.

B. Approved Charter of Schools

8. In 1903, the Qing government promulgated the "Approved charter of schools" and "Guimao schools system." It was the first school system which the Qing government has implemented in Chinese history. It established gymnastic class as a required course for all levels of schools. It has laid the sport's position in Chinese education. The regulation influenced the latter greatly.

C. To Train a New Army, and Run Affairs of State Schools

9. In 1903, the Government decreed to set up military training agency. In the following year, the Qing government promulgated two regulations for training the army and establishing overall levels of army schools. Various gymnastics training plays the most important role in various books and constitutions which are formulated and compiled by the army training department.

D. The Promotion of Normal Students of Every Province

10. In 1906, the Ministry of Education of Qing government ordered "the promotion of normal students of every province" to develop physical education learning. The orders solved the social conflicts of the acute shortage of teachers during the rapid development of new schools and laid the basis of Chinese physical teachers' education.

2. *See* http://www.zjj.gov.cn/website/xxgk/22/201007087396.shtml.

II. The Important Sports Event of Qing Government

11.

Left above: riding and shooting, Right above: wrestling, Left below: students doing physical exercises in a class break, Right below: drilling new soldiers.[3]

§2. The Development of Sports Law of the Republic of China

I. Overall Situation of Sports Law of the Republic of China

12. In 1911, Xinhai Revolution ended the era of China's feudal monarchy and established the Republic of China. China entered a new historical period. The legal system has also developed correspondingly.

13. In the early Republic of China, the government implemented some new regulations. In the sports field, the new regulations were endeavored to incorporate the physical education to the education reform. Until 1913, the school system then stipulated the requirement of gymnastic in different levels of schools. In 1914, the government published the "Ministry of Education Bureaucracy," provided that the Social Education Department of Ministry of Education is responsible for "matters of public sports and games." It has not set up a special sports administration yet.

3. *Source*: http://blog.sina.com.cn/s/blog_5e7f2b6e0100tvl6.html.

In 1915, the Congress made the martial arts a part of the school sports. In November 1922, the "school system reform order" developed a new system. In 1923, the "new academic curriculum standards" renamed the school's "gymnastics" to "Physical Education". This is not only a big reform in Chinese school physical education but also a big progress in the history of modern Chinese sports.

14. In 1928, the KMT government in Nanjing was established in China. China's special sports law has been gradually improved during this period. In 1929, the National Government announced the "National Sports Law", which had thirteen articles in total and ruled sporting purposes, methods, administrative organizations, sports organizations and teachers' qualifications. This is the first professional law about sports in China's history. In 1941 the National Government has announced a "Revised National Sports Law." With the two "National Sports Law," the KMT government has also developed guidelines on the implementation, such as the 1932 "National Sports Plan, 1941 "National Sports Policy Implementation," and 1945 "National Implementation Plan for Sports".

During that period, the national sports administration and the Ministry of Education are responsible for the sports management. The Education Ministry in 1927 established a "Sports Steering Committee" and "National Sports Plan" was published in 1932, which provided the establishment of Sports Commission of Education Ministry as the highest sports administration. In 1936, Physical Education Section Committee under the Ministry of Education was established as a sports administration organization. In 1945, upon the passing by the legislature, the National Government approved the "National Sports Committee Organization Regulations". It was then the establishment of sport administration had a full legal basis.

15. In total, the laws and regulations on the sports were systematic and complete. The National Sports Committee Organization had formulated and promulgated a number of sports laws, regulations and resolutions covering the basic sports law, sports organizations law, school sports law, social sports law, etc.

II. The Important Sports Event of the Republic of China

16. Left: Liu Changchun, famous Chinese sprinter, was part of the Chinese sports delegation that went for the first time to the 10th Olympic Games in Los Angeles in 1932. And he was the first person to appear on behalf of China in the world sports stage who proclaimed to the world that: the Olympics, Chinese are coming.

Right above: Football, Right below: Men's Pole Vault in National Games.[4]

4. *Source*: http://roll.sohu.com/20111018/n322612940.shtml.

§3. The Development of Sports Law of the People's Republic of China

I. Overall Situation of Sports Law of the People's Republic of China

17. In 1949, the People's Republic of China (PRC) established a new socialist legal system on sports with Chinese characteristics. This period can be divided into three stages.

From 1949 to 1976, it was the initial stage of development. Since the PRC was just founded, the State attached great importance to sports and regarded it as an important task for the government, and provided a range of protection from the organizational, institutional and legal aspects.

From 1966 to 1976, due to the chaos of "Cultural Revolution," sports have been seriously damaged like all walks, and the sports legal system was basically at a standstill.

18. From 1976 to 1995, it was the rapid development stage. After the Cultural Revolution, China's development has entered a new phase in 1978; China formally established the economic construction of the reform and opening-up policy. With China's rapid modernization and development of democracy and legal construction progress, construction of sports and sports law has entered a new stage of rapid development. During this period, the newly enacted laws and regulations covering almost all sports fields such as mass sports, competitive sports, school sports, education and culture provided a more comprehensive legal protection. In August 29, 1995, the fifth plenary session of the Eighth National People's Congress (NPC) passed *Sports Law of China*, which built a new milestone in China's sports.

From 1996 to the present, it is the full development stage. The enactment of *Law of the People's Republic China on Physical Culture and Sports* made China's sports legal system go to a fast developing era, especially the successful bid of Beijing Olympic Games greatly promoted China's legal construction of sports development. After 2001, in line with the organization of the Olympic Games, China carried out a series of legislation in national and local levels.

19. Until December 31, 2010, China had one sports law and eight sports regulations, which means China has initially formed the socialist sports legal system with Chinese characteristics. The post-Olympic sports law is still on the way in the direction of the reform and development of China's sports, to provide legal safeguard to build a powerful sports nation.

II. The Important Sports Event of the People's Republic of China

A. Xu Won the First Gold Medal for China in Olympic Games

20. Xu Haifeng (August 1, 1957—), Olympic champion, member of Chinese National Shooting Team, is the champion of Men's 50 meter pistol and the first gold winner of 23rd Olympics Games. Xu won the first gold medal for China in Olympic Games and became the first person to break China's "zero record" in Olympic gold medals. After becoming a coach, he has assisted other competitors to win two gold medals in Olympic Games. Xu is both a gold athlete and a gold coach.[5]

B. China Women's National Volleyball Team's Five Consecutive World Titles

21. China Women's National Volleyball Team won its first World Cup in 1981 and won the champion of World Women's Volleyball Championship in 1982 in Peru. In 1984, the team won the championship in Olympics held at Los Angeles. In 1985, the team won the World Cup again and won the champion of World Women's Volleyball Championship again in 1986. In 1986, while facing with many difficulties, the team was rewarded with the champion after winning all eight games and became the first team who took five consecutive World titles in the world volleyball history.[6]

5. *Source*: http://www.baike.com/wiki/%E8%AE%B8%E6%B5%B7%E5%B3%B0.
6. *Source*: http://news.k618.cn/history/pic/201608/t20160809_8557932.htm?p=5&s=false&qb=null.

C. China National Table Tennis Team Rocks the World

22. China National Table Tennis Team was founded in 1952 and experienced a progress from weak to strong and then lasted flourishing. China National Table Tennis Team which is inclusive of Men's and Women's Team has won many medals in international games and was named as Dream Team. After winning the gold medals of men's singles, women's singles, men's teams and women's teams in Beijing Olympics in 2008, China National Table Tennis Team was awarded champions in all four categories again.[7]

7. Picture source: https://baike.baidu.com/pic/%E4%B8%AD%E5%9B%BD%E4%B9%92%E4%B9%93%E7%90%83%E9%98%9F/8692693.

D. The 29th Beijing Olympic Games Was Successfully Held in Beijing

23. The 29th Summer Olympic Games was opened at 20 o'clock in the evening of August 8, 2008 in Beijing, Capital of China and was closed on August 24, 2008. A total of more than 60,000 athletes (11,438), coaches and officials from 204 countries or areas competed in 28 sports and 302 events. There were 43 world records and 132 Olympic records set at the Olympics. An unprecedented 86 countries won at least one medal during the Games. Chinese athletes won the most gold medals, with 51 and became the first Asian nation in Olympic history who leads the medals table.[8]

8. Picture source: http://2008.olympic.cn/.

E. Liu Xiang: Winner of Hurdles Grand Slam

24. Liu Xiang (July 13, 1983—), a famous track and field athlete, an Olympic Gold medalist and Champion of World Championships and World Indoor Championships, and an 110 meter hurdler with international level in China Men's Track and Field Team. Liu is a monumental person in the history of China track and field event. He is the first and the only athlete who achieved the "quadruple crown" of athletics: World Record Holder, World Champion, World Indoor Championship and Olympic Champion. While participating actively in charities, Liu has contributed a lot to the development of China sports and public services.[9]

9. Picture source: https://baike.baidu.com/pic/%E5%88%98%E7%BF%94/5836.

F. Li Na: Super Star in World Tennis HistoryF. Li Na: Super Star in World Tennis History

25. Li Na, the first and only Tennis Grand Slam singles champion from Asia, achieved the best ranking of Women's single of Asia. At the Australian Open in 2011, where she reached her first Grand Slam singles final and won the runner-up. In the same year, Li won her first major title at the French Open. Li was also the runner-up at the 2013 WTA Tour Championships. At the Australian Open, Li went into the finals for the third time and won the Australian Open champion on January 25, 2014. However, Li announced her retirement from the professional tennis on September 19, 2014.[10]

10. Picture source: https://baike.baidu.com/pic/%E6%9D%8E%E5%A8%9C/5285.

G. China Sports StarsG. China Sports Stars

26. Since China sent her first team to compete in Olympics in 1984 and Xu Haifeng won the shooting gold medal and became the first Olympic Champion of China, the dream of a world sports power arose from Chinese. Though, only five gold medals were obtained in 1988, we were aware of the gap between world sports nations. Through hard work, Chinese athletes made lots of progress. China won sixteen gold medals both in Barcelona and Atlantic Olympic Games, then won twenty-eight gold medals in Sydney and thirty-two gold medals in Athens where they ranked 2nd in gold medals table. In 2008, China ranked first in the gold medals table with fifty-one gold medals in Beijing. China has made remarkable achievements both of national power and social undertakings.

3154

Chapter 3. Sources of Sports Law

27. Contemporary Chinese sports law includes five main sources of law, namely, Constitution, legislation, administrative rules and regulations, local laws and regulations, and international treaties and international customs.

§1. Constitution

28. Constitution is the fundamental law formulated by the NPC. In the sources of law of China, the Constitution has the highest legal status and legal effect. All the laws, regulations and legislations are based on it. There are many constitutional articles on sports. Mainly in these areas: sports should adhere to and implement the principles and spirit of the law, the basic tasks and priorities of sports, the basic legal norms on sports. For example, Article 22 of the Constitution of the PRC: "The state develops physical culture and promotes mass sports activities to improve the people's physical fitness."

§2. Legislation

29. Legislation here is narrowly defined, which refers to the legal documents formulated by the NPC and its Standing Committee. Its legal status and legal effect are only second to the Constitution, and also an important source of sports law. According to the different formulation organs, it can be divided into the basic law and non-basic law. Besides, Law of the People's Republic China on Physical Culture and Sports is the basic Chinese sports law, which contains sports' status, tasks, objectives, basic principles, social sports, school sports, competitive sports, the sports industry, sports exchanges, legal liability and so on. In addition to the above, there are still many relevant legal provisions.

§3. Administrative Rules and Regulations

30. Administrative rules and regulations are developed and released by the state administrative organs, and its effectiveness is lower than the Constitution and the law. Based on the different formulation organs, they are divided into administrative rules and administrative regulations. A large number of such rules and regulations form the main sources of sports law.

§4. Local Laws and Regulations

31. Local laws and regulations are issued by the local state authorities to ensure the compliance and enforcement of the Constitution, laws and administrative regulations, combined with the actual situation in the region. Its effectiveness is lower than the Constitution, laws and administrative regulations, and the effectiveness of local regulations is lower than local regulations. Article 100 of Constitution of PRC: "The people's congresses of provinces and municipalities directly under the Central Government and their standing committees may adopt local regulations, which must not contravene the Constitution and the law and administrative rules and regulations, and they shall report such local regulations to the Standing Committee of the National People's Congress for the record." China has many such local laws and regulations, such as *Administrative Measures of Shanghai Sports Venues*, the effect of local laws and regulations are limited to the area.

§5. International Treaties and International Customs

32. In the era of globalization, sports are also becoming global. China has a lot of treaties with foreign countries, according to the principle of "Pacta sunt servanda." In addition to reservations outside the international treaty, China is legally bound. For example, International Covenant on Civil and Political Rights, International Covenant on Economic Social and Cultural Rights.

International customs should get the recognition of international community and the sports community. The application of international customs shall not violate the public interests of the PRC. Chinese domestic law sets the effect of international treaties and international conventions. For example, Article 142 of General Principles of the Civil Law of the PRC: "The application of law in civil relations with foreigners shall be determined by the provisions in this CHAPTER. If any international treaty concluded or acceded to by the People's Republic of China contains provisions differing from those in the civil laws of the People's Republic of China, the provisions of the international treaty shall apply, unless the provisions are ones on which the People's Republic of China has announced reservations. International practice may be applied to matters for which neither the law of the People's Republic of China nor any international treaty concluded or acceded to by the People's Republic of China has any provisions."

Part I. Organization of Sport

33. With the rapid development of the society, the community gradually comes into people's horizons. Since the 1980s, "community revolution" has begun to emerge in the global scope. It relieved the governmental dilemma that social problems became more expanded and complicated than ever, which not only provided a new vision for social management, also promoted the political, economic and cultural pace on democratization. Since China's reform and opening, establishing the socialist market economy system has been the core objective of China. It also marked the past planned economy under the government management model and had completed its task in the history, therefore the power in social fields decentralized, gradually forming a dualistic social management structure of the government and the society. Being the main organizational form of social sports management function, sports organization gradually formed a relatively mature system.

Chapter 1. General Issues

§1. The Development of Organization of Sport

34. Since antiquity, sport has played an important part of human society, not only because of the benefit it brings to health, but also the enjoyment of it. And many organizations of sport contributed a lot to the development of sport at that time in Chinese history. The organizations of sport had a great development in Song dynasty.[11] There were many famous and big Wushu organizations such as "Jiaodi community," "Yinglue community," "Jinbiao community," "Qiyun community," a Cuju community which had existed during the reigns of three emperors, had promoted the development of Chinese football for hundred years; many varied non-government secret community which combined through activities like alignment, missionary, Wushu practice had appeared and promoted sport activities doggedly when different races ruled in Qing dynasty. It suggests that organization of sport is a need of society and an objective exist. In the modern society, western athletic sports came into China and a lot of organizations of sport showed up, like Datong Athletic Association, South China Athletic Association, Songkou Athletic Association, Chin Woo Athletic Association, Chinese Warrior Society, Beijing Sport Competition and Improvement Society, China National Amateur Athletic Federation, and Shanghai Glides Gracefully Sports Club. In revolution base area, organizations of sport, including Lenin Club, Red Athletic Association, Yanan Athletic Association, and Yanan New Sport Association, had efficiently organized sports activities during the revolutionary war.[12]

After New China was founded, organizations of sport had gone through three fastigiums, the first was in 1956 when seventeen national organizations of sport established in this year (Table 1).

Table 1 Established in 1956[13]

Organization Name	*Established Time*
Chinese Basketball Association	October 1956
Chinese Volleyball Association	Same as above
Chinese Athletics Association	Same as above
Chinese Swimming Association	Same as above
Chinese Gymnastics Association	Same as above

11. Zhou Weiliang, *Research in Secret Association of Martial Arts Activities in the Qing Dynasty*, 4 J. Chendu Chengdu Sports University 1 (1991).
12. Lu Yuanzhen, *Theory of the Chinese Sports Community*, 1 J. Beijing Sport U. 2 (1996).
13. Huang Yaling, *Theory of the Chinese Sports Community - The Sports Community Reform under the Transformational Relation Between Nation and Society*, Ph.D. Thesis 34 (Beijing Sport University 2003).

Chinese Table Tennis Association	Same as above
Chinese Badminton Association	Same as above
Chinese Shooting Association	Same as above
Chinese Tennis Association	Same as above
Chinese Weightlifting Association	Same as above
Chinese Boxing Association	Same as above
Chinese Wrestling Association	Same as above
Chinese Cycling Association	Same as above
Chinese Football Association	Same as above
The Chinese Association of Dong Yun (Chinese Ice Hockey Association, Chinese Skating Association, Chinese Skiing Association, Chinese Snowmobiles Association, Chinese Sled sports Association)	Established in 1956, divided into five association in 1979
Chinese Water Conservancy and Electricity Sports Association	Established in June 30, 1956, divided into Chinese Water Conservancy Sports Association and Chinese Electricity Sports Association in 1992
Chinese Public Security Sports Association	Established in 1956, changed to Chinese avant-garde sports association in 1958

35. After the founding of new China, the government cleaned up and rectified the organizations of sport, and made the original sports public welfare social organizations, sports organizations, sports associations and sports academic community carry on the registration in accordance with the law. The government assured its valid legal status, and cleaned up feudalistic and superstitious sports organizations. It enacted Interim Measures for Registration of Social Organizations in September 1950. Then, "Detailed Rules for the Implementation of Interim Measures for Registration of Social Organizations" is laid down to guide the practice in March 1953. Chinese economy had gone through depression during 1959–1961, and it played a big impact on the development of organization of sport. The related data indicated that no organization of sport established in this three years. The development of organization of sport went back on track because of the recovery of national economy in 1962. The second fastigium appeared in 1964 and eight national organizations of sport were established in this year (Table 2).

Table 2 Established in 1964[14]

Organization Name	*Established Time*
Chinese Marine Model Sports Association	Established in February 3, 1964
Chinese Aero sports Association	Same as above
Chinese Radio Sports Association	Same as above
Chinese Chess Association	Same as above
Chinese Weiqi Association	Same as above
Chinese Archery Association	Same as above
Chinese Wushu Association	Same as above
Chinese Sports Philately Association	Same as above

36. The reform and opening-up policy had brought new energy to the development of organization of sport in 1978, and the third fastigium appeared after a one-year chrysalis. thirteen national organizations of sport established in 1979, which is a year later since the foundation of the country (Table 3).

Table 3 Established in 1979[15]

Organization Name	*Established Time*
Chinese Baseball and Softball Association	Established in March 9, 1979, divided into Chinese Baseball Association and Softball Association in 1983
Chinese Handball Association	Established in March 9, 1979
Chinese Judo Association	Established in December 27, 1979
Chinese Motor Sports Association	Established in March 9, 1979
Chinese Modern Pentathlon Winter Two Association	Established in December 27, 1979
Chinese Equestrian Association	Same as above
Chinese Fencing Association	Established in March 9, 1979
Chinese Sports Press Association	Established in December 27, 1979
Chinese Yachting Association	Established in March 9, 1979
Chinese Canoeing Association	Same as above
Chinese Boating Association	Same as above
Chinese School Sports Association	Same as above

14. Huang Yaling, *Theory of the Chinese Sports Community - The Sports Community Reform under the Transformational Relation Between Nation and Society*, Ph.D. Thesis 35 (Beijing Sport University 2003).
15. Huang Yaling, *Theory of the Chinese Sports Community - The Sports Community Reform under the Transformational Relation Between Nation and Society*, Ph.D. Thesis 36 (Beijing Sport University 2003).

Chinese Bridge Association	Established in September 29, 1979

37. After the reform and opening-up policy, the sports industry showed vigorous development trend with the deepening reform of economic system. In addition to actively participating in various international specifications of sports, the domestic competition among the various professional leagues became the main growth point of sports industry. The organizations on the basis of this growth gradually stabilized, and the development was mainly concentrated toward the business aspect of sport. As of April 2016, affiliated state general administration of sports in China is 77, the number of national sport associations with the Olympic project are thirty-one and there are thirty-six non-Olympic sports.[16]

§2. Concept of Organization of Sport

38. From the point of the present study, on the concept that organization of sport did not form a unified expression, the relevant legal documents did not provide a clear definition on it, so the scholars of the concept of organization of sport study are on the premise of the understanding of the concept of organization. In general, organization refers to social groups, also known as "associations," and represents institutions of the organization of society which differs from the mandatory state agencies. The relatively consistent opinions suggest that the understanding of organization is ought to be consistent with the elements of nonprofit organization "structure operation," as Salamon (1981) proposed, which must meet the following conditions: (1) Organized, a certain degree of institutionalization; (2) Private, differs from the government agencies; (3) Nonprofit, managers and owners are not to profit from organization; (4) Autonomy, independent transaction; (5) Voluntary, accept the participation of volunteers.[17] Regulation on Registration and Administration of Social Organizations, issued in 1989, did not give a straight definition of organization, but listed "association, institute, joint association, seminar, foundation, promotion association, chamber of commerce" included in the category of society. However, the first paragraph of Article 2 of the Regulation (issued in 1998, amended in 2016) made a definition of community in the form of law for the first time: "Social organization" referred to these regulations constituted of Chinese citizens of voluntary, common aspiration for the realization of the members, in accordance with its articles of association to carry out the activities of nonprofit social groups. Its second paragraph points out that organizations rather the government agency can be unit member to join the nonprofit organization. Based on the limits of the nonprofit organization and the definition of community in our country's legal concepts, scholars discussed the concept of "organizations of sport": (1) Through the literature retrieval, the earliest scholar on the research of organizations of sport is Lu Yuanzhen (1995); he suggests that an organization of sport is a social

16. Website of General Administration of Sports, http://www.sport.gov.cn/index.html, on April 20, 2016.
17. Li Yaping, *The Rise of the Third Domain – Writings on Western Volunteer Work and Volunteer Organization Theory* 33–35 (Fudan University Press 1998).

organization whose goal or activity is primarily sports;[18] (2) Professor Huang Yalin suggests that organizations of sport are constituted of citizens of voluntarism, self-awareness, to achieve the common aspiration of members, in accordance with its articles of association to carry out the activities of nonprofit social groups;[19] (3) Professor Ye Guoxiong agrees with Gu Yuanyan's opinion to limit the elements to define organizations of sport, which must meet the following conditions: "1. at least 2 members and mutually accept; 2. different degree of the common interested content or goal of sports; 3. stable and persistent interaction; 4. Participate in unified activities frequently; 5. behavioral norms and restriction of accepting norms; 6. the members of organizations of sport have a partner consciousness for achieving the same goal";[20] (4) Doctor Zhang Zhenlong thinks that an organization of sport is constituted of citizens of voluntary, with the goals that promote or develop sport, in accordance with its articles of association to carry out the activities of nonprofit social groups.[21]

39. To define a concept, the first thing is to reveal the essential property of this thing; the second thing is that defined item cannot be defined again; the third thing is that the expression of concept is brief and precise.[22] The definition of organizations of sport should be done in two steps. At the first, on the understanding of "organization," the legal definition given by "Regulations Governing the Registration of Social Organization" is fairly comprehensive, so we can adopt this definition as the framework of the definition of organizations of sport. Second, we should discuss the essential property of organizations of sport on the basis of sport. The problem of opinion (1) is that defined item cannot be a definition entry. The problem of opinion (3) is that it is not brief and precise enough. The opinion (2) and opinion (4) have divergence in some parts: No. 1, "managed in self-awareness" is whether a necessary definition entry; No. 2, "to achieve the common aspiration of members" is whether a necessary definition entry; No. 3, how to reflect the essential property of "organizations of sport." The reason for adding "managed in self-awareness" into the definition in opinion (2) is that legal definition is lack of non-governmental and autonomy, two essential properties.[23] In fact, the contents of "voluntary," "common aspiration of members," "in accordance with its articles of association" in this legal definition have already expressed non-governmental and autonomy. Exclusion of the state organs in the second paragraph is stressed about this, so the element of "managed in self-awareness" can be omitted. Opinion (4) has omitted "to achieve the common aspiration of members," and combined sport and the omitted content by "with the goals that promote or develop sport". The expression is brief enough, but too narrow. Although scholars express as precisely as

---

18. Lu Yuanzhen, *Theory of the Chinese Sports Community*, 1 J. Beijing Sport U. 1–2 (1996).
19. Huang Yaling, *Theory of the Chinese Sports Community - The Sports Community Reform under the Transformational Relation Between Nation and Society*, Ph.D. Thesis 30 (Beijing Sport University 2003).
20. Ye Guoxiong & Liu Yuanxiang, *Sports Club in China*, 1 J. Shandong Sports U. 2 (2008).
21. Zhang Zhenlong, *Legal System of Our Country Sports Club Basic Research*, Ph.D. Thesis 5 (Beijing Sport University 2012).
22. Ma Kechang, *Hundreds of Crime Theory* 1219 (Peking University Press 2014).
23. Huang Yaling, *Theory of the Chinese Sports Community - The Sports Community Reform under the Transformational Relation Between Nation and Society*, Ph.D. Thesis 29 (Beijing Sport University 2003).

they can, not all organizations of sport are with the goals that promote or develop sport, there are also some academic and research organizations.

In conclusion, we give the definition in this article: organizations of sport is a nonprofit organization which is constituted of Chinese citizens of voluntary, and the common interest of its members is to develop or carry out sport activities in accordance with its articles of association.

§3. Classification of Organizations of Sport

40. The classification of the organizations of sport results in different results based on different classification standards. Classification method of organizations of sport currently adopted by the scholars mainly has the following kinds: (1) according to four benchmarks that the forming process of the organization, the generation of leadership, the identity of the main leaders and source of financial support, Wang Yin has classified organizations of sport into government-run, half government-run and half civilian-run, civilian-run;[24] (2) Wan Li and Luo Lin have used the classification of the organizations from the prospect of legality of Gao Bingzhong for reference, classified organizations of sport into social legality of the organizations of sport, administrative legality of the organizations of sport, political legality of the organizations of sport and law legality of the organizations of sport;[25] (3) Lu Yuanzhen comprehensively has considered the service type and function of the organizations of sport and classified organizations of sport into organizations of competitive sports, organizations of social sports, organizations of sports science academic, organizations of sports audience, organizations of sports news, organizations of sport of enjoyment, sports chamber of commerce;[26] (4) Professor Huang Yalin has used the classification of nonprofit organization of Professor Wang Min for reference, and classified organizations of sports into organizations with membership system and organizations with non-membership system, and classified organizations with membership system into mutual benefit organizations of sports, public welfare organizations of sports and regulatory organizations of sports;[27] (5) Liu Xinran, Wang Xuanhe, Liu Hanyang adopted five different standards to classify organizations of sports, including: according to the relationship with government, it can be classified top-down and bottom-up; according to the relationship with market, it can be classified profit and nonprofit; according to the relationship with society, it can be classified voluntary, public welfare and welfare; according to the relationship with sports, it can be classified supporting mass sports development and supporting competitive sports development; according to the relationship with public service products, it can be classified into the nonprofit

24. Wang Ying, Zhe Xiaoye and Sun Yaobing, *Middle Layer Society: Reform and Social Organizations in China* 15 (China Development Press 1993).
25. Wan Li & Luo Ling, *The Legitimacy of the Sports Community Classification and Development Countermeasures*, 2 J. Beijing Sport U. 155–157 (1996).
26. Lu Yuanzhen, *Sports Sociology* 46 (Beijing Sport University Press 2000).
27. Huang Yaling, *Theory of the Chinese Sports Community - The Sports Community Reform under the Transformational Relation Between Nation and Society*, Ph.D. Thesis 31 (Beijing Sport University 2003).

organization of sport for product supply and nonprofit organization of sport for intermediary services.[28]

To classify organization of sport reasonably, some necessary principles need to be confirmed: first, the object to be classified must meet the definition of "organization of sport;" second, the adopted standard must cover all objects which meet the definition; third, the types under a standard must be mutually exclusive, which means one object can only be classified to one certain type in a certain standard.

41. According to those principles, opinion (1) violates the point that organization of sport should keep independence relative to government agencies; opinion (2) violates the mutually exclusive principle, because all organization of sport can be classified into all types at the same time in current system, and all legality can be one; opinion (3) has the same problem as opinion (2); opinion (5) violates the essential property of nonprofit of organization of sport. So opinion (4) is more reasonable in classification standard, and we adopt opinion (4) (Figure 1)

Figure 1 Classification of Organization of Sport

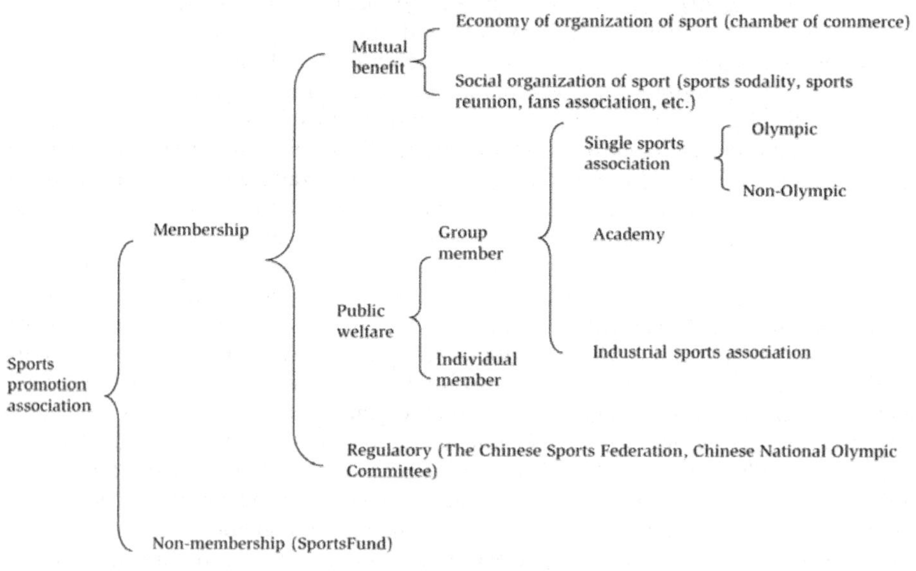

28. Liu Xinran, Wang Xuanhe and Liu Hanyang, *Sports Non-profit Organization and Its Role in Modern Society*, 1 J. Jilin Inst. Physical Educ. 18–19 (2007).

Chapter 2. Public Regulation

§1. FREEDOM OF ASSOCIATION

I. The Connotation of the Freedom of Association

42. Freedom of association means citizens should be free to organize or participate in a sustainable association according to certain purposes and legal procedures. Freedom of association is second only to the individual's freedom of behavior—one of the most basic freedom, which is non-transferable as well as personal freedom. From the perspective of the Chinese Constitution in Article 35:

> Citizens of the People's Republic of China enjoy freedom of speech, of the press, of assembly, of association, of procession and of demonstration.

43. Yu Xingzhong thinks that the connotation of the freedom of association includes four aspects. First, citizens should enjoy freedom of choosing their goal and pursuing the common ideal when forming an association, namely substantive freedom. Second, freedom of association also refers to people in the community enjoy formal freedom, including the size of the community, the choice of the name, organization setting, etc. Again, freedom of association also means that people are free to express on associating or not. Finally, freedom of association also applies to communities that can freely make decision about affairs of themselves.[29]

44. From the connotation identified, the last aspect is controversial. The existence scope of freedom of association shall be limited before citizens (including legal persons of non-state organ) have organized or participated in a community. Community's freedom of decision-making on their affairs should belong to the category of community autonomy. The autonomy is on the basis of freedom of association, but not equivalent. In addition, the general meaning of freedom contains dual meaning of positive and negative. It cannot only be praised and pursued but also be refused and boycott state, so special instruction on express way is unnecessary. Therefore connotation of social freedom should include two aspects: the substance and the form. The substance of freedom refers to citizens enjoying the freedom of choice in their goal when they join or form a community. The form of freedom lies in the fact that citizens shall have the right to make decision on a community's name, purpose, size, structure, etc.

29. Yu Xingzhong, *Consultative Democracy and Freedom of Association*, Corporate Legal Environment Seminar (2003).

II. Restrictions on Freedom of Association

45. Obviously, the connotation of the statement is without considering constraints, freedom of association is still affected by many restrictions in China. The relationship between restrictions on freedom of association and the safeguard is a unity of opposites. If the clarity of guarantee is not expressed legally, it will merely become a formality. In contrast, if the abuse of right is not limited, the guarantee of freedom will be impossible. Chinese scholars have given a lot of attention to the limitation of freedom of association. Li Long and Xia Li'an sum up the restrictions in three aspects: entity, procedural, and restriction on the legal person status.[30] Liu Peifeng suggests, freedom of association should be limited, mainly in specific person, specific types of association and association ban, etc.[31] Having summed up the European court judicial precedents, Chen Xinxin considers that restrictions on freedom of association must be "limitation of law," and must be a legally established by a legal purpose, and is an "essential of democratic society," which must meet the principle of proportionality to keep balance between the urgent needs of society, the extent of limitation and the goal of society. Due to the possible ambiguity of law, the scope and exercise of discretion shall be specifically limited in full, in order to protect the individual from arbitrary interference.[32]

46. At present, "Prevention" model is the main way of social organization management in China. Moreover, dual licensing system is used in administrative supervision, which means the establishment of sports communities should be approved by the Civil Affairs Department (CAD) and Sports Administrative Department (SAD). First paragraph of Article 3 of the Regulation on Registration and Administration of Social Organizations has made a general provision:

> To become established, social organizations must be approved by the authorized department [zhuguan danwei] and follow the registration procedure set out in these regulations.

Similar rules in Article 9:

> Candidate social organizations must be investigated and approved [shencha] by a professional leading unit, and applying persons [faqi ren] must make preliminary application to the registration and management agency.

Analyzing the research above, the restrictions are mainly manifested in several aspects:

(1) Restriction on subject. Though state personnel does not have any specific limit of association, state organs have. According to the second paragraph of Article 2 in the Regulation:

30. Li Long and Xia Li'an, *The Right of Freedom of Association*, 12 Leg. Sci. 6–7 (1997).
31. Liu Peifeng, *Community Legislation of the European Union Countries: A Preliminary Introduction*, 3 Global L. Rev. 287–294 (2004).
32. Chen Xinxin, *Judicial Guarantee of Freedom of Association*, 3 Global L. Rev. 273–286 (2004).

All groups other than state organs may join social organizations as institutional members.

(2) Substantial restrictions. In the establishment stage, CAD and SAD will perform their duties on audit of purpose and category of the community. According to the first paragraph of Article 4 in the Regulation:

> Social organizations must observe the constitution, state laws, regulations and state policy, and must not oppose the basic principles of the constitution, harm the unity, security or ethnic harmony of the state, or interests of the state and society, or the lawful interests of other organizations or citizens, or offend social morality.

So if the aim of a community is in violation of the provisions, it cannot be approved, and could even be considered as an illegal organization.

(3) Formal restrictions. The formal restrictions on sports organization reflect in number of membership, name, organization structure, residence, personnel, funds, as well as civil subject qualification, etc. This can be seen from the related provisions of the Regulations:

> Article 10
>
> To establish a social organization the following conditions must be satisfied:
>
> A. An organization must have more than 50 individual members or more than 30 institutional members or, if it has both individual and institutional members, a total of at least fifty.
>
> B. It must have a standard name, and organizational capacity.
>
> C. It must have a fixed location.
>
> D. It must have staff with qualifications appropriate to the professional activities of the organization.
>
> E. It must have lawful assets and a source of funds. National level organizations must have a minimum of 100,000 yuan to cover their activities; local social organizations and inter-area social organizations must have a minimum of 30,000 yuan.

F. It must be legally liable in its own right.

A social organization's name must comply with the law and statutory regulations and must not offend public morality. A social organization's name must reflect its activities, character and area of operations. Where national organizations use 'Chinese',

'All-China' etc, in their titles, they must be approved in accordance with the relevant state regulations. Local social organizations cannot use 'National', 'Chinese', 'All China' etc. in their names.

§2. Governmental Conditions and Permits

I. Sports Public Policies in China

47. In general, the policy refers to the political conduct and action rules of state organs, political parties and other political groups, which is in order to achieve and serve the goal of a certain social, economic, and cultural politics in a specific period, and it is a series of strategies, decrees measures, approaches, methods, and regulations in general.[33] Sports public policy refers to regulation and guidelines on social organizations and individuals' behavior, which is to solve the main problems that happen during the developing process of public sports in a certain period.[34] The year 1995 was undoubtedly a very important mark of legalization for sports. Promulgated in that year, *Law of the People's Republic of China on Physical Culture and Sports* made a series of sports public policy and principles were put forward, which were related closely to the development of sports in China (Table 4).

Table 4 Premier Sports Public Policy 1995–2015

Name	*Year*	*Institution*	*Influence*
Sports Industry Development Program 1995–2010	1995	General Administration of Sport	Chinese sports industry will use fifteen years to gradually build a modern sports industry system: conforming with socialist market economic system, in line with modern sports law, wide range, reasonable structure, standardizing the developing normatively, and promoting the development of the socialist sports.

33. Chen Zhenming, *Policy Science* 59 (China Renmin University Press 1998).
34. Li Jie, *Study on the Implementation of Mass Sports Policy in Beijing City*, Ph.D. Thesis 6 (Fujian Normal University 2008).

Opinions on Accelerating Development and Strengthening Sports Clubs' Management	1999	General Administration of Sport	This advice is conducive to the establishment of the sports system that is fit for the socialist market economy, and it provides organizational security for implementation of the national fitness program and Olympic Glorious Program, and it helps to strengthen standardized management at same time, and it not only promotes the healthy development of sports clubs, but also strengthens the sports legal system and improves sports laws.
Sports Reform and Development Program 2001–2010	2000	the State Council	The Program promotes the development of competitive sports events which are advantageous, ensuring leadership of them in the international arena. Sports industry began to become social, scientific, industrial and legal, which has laid a solid foundation for basil sports modernization in the middle of new century.
Sports "Eleventh Five-Year" Plan	2006	General Administration of Sport	The Plan clearly puts forward the guiding ideology of the development of sports in the "Eleventh Five-Year" period: guided by the Scientific Outlook on Development, taking the opportunity of organizing 2008 Olympic Games, treating the growing demand of masses for sports culture as starting point and destination for all the work, aiming at improving the quality of health of the nation, providing policy support for hosting the 2008 Olympic Games.
Regulation on National Fitness	2009	the State Council	It triggers a national fitness craze and inspires enthusiasm of people for fitness activities, and it helps to ensure the right of citizens to participate in fitness activities, improving the physical fitness of citizens. While developing competitive sports, it encourages all people to participate in sports.

Guiding Opinions on Accelerating the Development of Sports Industry	2010	General Office of the State Council	It introduces a number of specific policies and measures to increase strength of investment and financing, and to improve tax incentives. It supports qualified sports enterprises to enter the capital market, broadening the financing channels for the sports industry. By actively encouraging private and foreign capital to invest in the sports industry for construction sports facilities, it stimulates the domestic surplus labor employment. It also encourages financial institutions to adapt to the development of sports industry needs, which develops new products and new business, promoting diversified development of the sports industry. It provides policy support for the development of sports industry and stimulates sports consumption.
National Fitness Program (2011–2015)	2011	the State Council	On the basis of the Regulation on National Fitness, the fitness activities receive more budget support, which stimulates the domestic sports industry, such as sports apparel and sports fitness industry. Much perfected system of preferential policies-financial, taxation, financial and land-guides and encourages the social forces for investments and donations, more investors are willing to fund the establishment of national fitness cause.
Sports Industry, "Twelfth Five-Year" Plan	2011	General Administration of Sport	It highlighted the problem that sports industry was still in a very low proportion of the national economy. It also increased investment and financing into the sports industry, and began to transform government functions that should focus on management. The Plan put forward innovative operation mechanism of stadiums, which promotes the separation between stadium ownership and management, and professional operation institutions of stadiums began to flourish. At the same time, the Plan emphasizes the establishment of the sports events band and the protection of sports intangibles, the concept of sports brands gained ground.

Separation of Management Reform Program in Chinese Football League	2012	Chinese Football Association	Deepening the Separation Reform in professional league, the Program shows full respect for all participates to make them function well, and it has set blueprint for the healthy developing mechanisms of the professional league. The Program has set up effective supervision and restriction on executive decision-making powers which weakens administrative intervention, so that the business operation mechanism of professional league is more transparent.
Several Opinions on Promoting the Development of Integration of Cultural Creative, Design Services and Related Industries	2014	the State Council	Cultural creativity industries and design-service activities are closely related to the primary, the secondary and the tertiary industries, and the sports industry has been identified as the key of them. Sports industry began to amalgamate with industries of the Cultural creativity and the design-service, which are high value-added. To gain long-term development of the sports industry, it further guides the sports competition show business and the development of sports services, while promoting sports derivatives design, which further promotes the development of related industries.
Deployment of Accelerating the Development of the Sports Industry and Promoting Sports Consumption by Public Fitness	2014	Executive Meetings of the State Council	It laid the foundation for the introduction of industry-related sports programming. Treated as a "special" industry, sports industry began to play a role in boost domestic demand and transformation of economic growth. It emphasizes the low level of industrialization of sports, where there is a huge development space. It also encourages the development of core industry of sports.
Opinions on Accelerating the Development of Sports Industry and Promoting Sports Consumption	2014	the State Council	It points out there is a huge potential market space of sports industry, which should be used for boosting domestic demand and promoting consumption, and the stocks related will usher in investment opportunities. It proposes to create a sports market worthy CNY 5 trillion by 2025.

General Plan of Reform and Development of Chinese Football	2015	the State Council	The Plan clearly puts forward the three objectives. Short-term: normative management system. Medium-term: competition level of professional league achieves the best in Asia; the national soccer team is near the top of Asia; women's returns to one of the world-class teams. Long-term: hosting the World Cup; soccer team reaches the World Cup and the Olympics.

48. Although, papers on sports public policy of 2016 are not published till now, the basic orientation has been finalized, which is divided into several areas:

(1) Football is a benchmark of sports reform. Following the General Plan of Reform and Development of Chinese Football and the Adjustment Plan of Reform and Development of Chinese Football, the task of separation between General Administration of Sport and Chinese Football has been completed, and the next to-do is to make additional details of division of functions, personnel, foreign affairs, party building and the governmental purchase of services.

(2) "Combination of Discharge tube" model is taken on Marathon matches, which need more reasonable policies and mechanism to make more social units, corporates and finance funds invest into Marathon and other mass sports activities.

(3) Creating "Made in China" sports products. Target of CNY 5 trillion makes sports industry become a gold mining for social capital, which means a huge space for development; therefore, it becomes crucially important to know how to activate, guide and regulate the development of the sports industry.

(4) Pulling the winter sports industry and strengthening international cooperation. Zhangjiakou, Beijing bids for Winter Olympic Games 2022 successfully, which will give the winter sports industry an unprecedented opportunity for development. However, China is still in an infantile stage of winter sports industry, which means a series of obstacles, such as site, talent and technology, etc. Therefore, it is imperative to combine China's capital market with developed countries' technology, personnel.

(5) Preparing for the Rio Olympics.

In summary, sports policies in China are generally divided into three categories, which have basically formed China's sports policy system:

(1) Aiming at improving the national health, meeting the public's demand for sports entertainment.

(2) Providing spiritual products of collective and national honor by sports competition.

(3) Promoting the development of sports industry.

II. Administrative Licensing

A. Mode of Administrative Supervision

49. Currently, a much comprehensively regulatory system is taken on China's sports associations. There are a lot of academic discussions on it. Wang Ming believes that there are two different management models of China's organizations, namely, the governmental selection and social selection.[35] Wu Yuzhang insists that it is governmental selection for management in China, which is a set of relatively fixed practices that the government implements in communities' establishment, activities, and revocation.[36] In fact, the way adopted for sports associations can be summarized as a management model of "centralized registration, double responsibility, and hierarchical management".[37]

"Centralized registration" and "double responsibility" refer to the "dual licensing" model mentioned previously, which means sports communities should build relationships with CADs and sports administration departments on the stage of establishment. There is a distribution of management between the two departments. CADs focus on managing register, macro guidance, supervision and inspection, and administrative departments of sports focus on providing direction on the operational activities and self-construction. However, the objectives of two departments are consistent. They both give development and management equal value and promote the healthy development of civil society organizations.

By "Hierarchical management," it means that national communities should register in national departments, and local ones should register in local departments that above country level. It does not mean that society has different grades, but that the source and scope of activities and members have been divided.

III. Details of Administrative Licensing

50. Before introducing the details of the administrative licensing of sports associations, three points must be explained:

(1) The current governmental regulation of the national sports associations was the Interim Measures for the National Sports Community Management, but there is no uniform standard for local sports organizations management. Local management measures modeled their content after the Interim Measures and contained a set of local color. Therefore, we will introduce administrative licensing of national sports associations as a typical.
(2) Because the supervision of Sports Association in business is very stringent, it contains a mass of specific administrative license. Due to the limit of space, we will introduce general administrative licensing items below.

35. Wang Ming, *Chinese Association Reform – From Governmental Choice to Social Choice* 64 (Social Sciences Academic Press 2001).
36. Wu Yuzhang, *Legal Problems of Association* 6 (Social Sciences Academic Press 2004).
37. Zhang Zhenlong, *Legal System of Our Country Sports Club Basic Research*, Ph.D. Thesis 93 (Beijing Sport University 2012).

(3) As the administrative licensing related to freedom of associations in establishment stage has been explained, the following is mainly about other aspects of it.

The Department of business administration issues licenses. The General Administration of Sport consists of nine departments, so the different issues involved will be approved by different agencies. Refer to the Interim Measures provisions:

Article 21

The following departments of the General Administration of Sport will be responsible for business guidance and management:

A. The Personnel Department in charge of personnel department is responsible for the review of establishment, institutional settings, change and the heads' qualification of community. The Sports Economic Department is responsible for the supervision of financial system, funds using, audit and operation of community. The External liaison department is responsible for the administration of foreign affairs. The Party Committee is responsible for the party affairs. The Supervision Bureau is responsible for the punishment for illegal behavior and violation of community with civil affairs departments and judicial authority.

B. Other departments, divisions and bureaus implement centralized management of community according to their main function.

51. In the management of the national sports associations, in addition to the daily business, the Interim Measures set approval and filing systems for foreign affairs, annual review, and major conference:

Article 22

The following factors of communities shall be applied for approval or recorded by the General Administration of sport or relevant departments:

A. The annual summary and work plan shall be reported to the General Administration of Sport for the filing.

B. Arrangements of Foreign activities or other major events shall be reported to the General Administration of Sport for approval. Congresses and members meetings and other important meetings shall be submitted to the State Sports

General Administration agreed, and sports industry associations shall be reported to the General Administration of Sport for the filing.

52. Because the nature of the society is unprofitable, the relationship between communities and other economic entities is under the strict control of the relevant departments, which can be read from the Interim Measures:

Article 23

The economic entities invested in by communities shall be examined and approved by the Sports Economic Department and shall register with the relevant departments. In business activities entities engaged in, income belonging to communities shall be fully used for the development of communities' causes. Associations shall not engage in profit-making business activities. Without the approval of the General Administration of Sport, associations shall not be engaged in all kinds of economic entities affiliated.

53. For the significant impact of national sports associations, relevant departments have stringent requirements of personnel, especially for leading members. According to the Interim Measures, leading members refer to:

Article 31

The composition of the members of community leadership organization should not only consider the universality and representative, but also carry out the principle of efficient and effective. According to the specific circumstances, it generally includes: standing committee 7-19 people, chairman (director, president) 1 people, vice chairman (vice director, vice president) 5-15 people, the secretary-general 1 people, deputy secretary-general 1-5 people, Guest posts served by personnel who have sponsored are not subject to this restriction.

When the above personnel need to change, communities should apply for approval of relevant departments with due procedures, which refer to:

Paragraph 2 of Article 31

Elected by collective members or representatives of groups, community leaders represent interests of their group, which should be changed with the change of personnel. After candidates recommended by their groups, the personnel changes should be applied for approval of the Personnel Department in form of suggestion of the unit to which the Secretariat of the association belongs.

In addition, the relevant conditions of the leadership refer to:

Article 32

Community leaders composed of experts and scholars who are related to community business, leaderships of sports administrative departments, representatives of sports and relevant administrative departments, and businessmen who support community enthusiastically. Generally, the personnel mentioned above are in post but for special need, even so, the age of them should under 70 years old. For longtime leaderships who have made outstanding contributions, they can be awarded honorary chairman(honorary director, honorary president), honorary vice chairman (honorary vice director, honorary vice president) and honorary consultant when they leave service. According to the procedure, the investiture should follow the recommendation of the group affiliated by the association and the approval of the General Administration of Sport for which the relevant functional departments applied after ratification. Honorary member are decided according to the Articles of association except the All-China Sports Federation and the Chinese Olympic Committee.

54. Establishment of branch. In the past, the dual management system had applied to establishment of sports association branches, but after modification of the Regulation on Registration and Administration of Social Organizations in 2016, it deleted articles related to the CADs, which made the SADs become the only competent authorities. Specific items of it are regulated in paragraphs 1, 2 of Article 17 of the Regulation and paragraphs 2, 3, 4 of Article 25 of the Interim Measures. The following should be noted:

(1) Branches and representative agencies are parts of the social group. They are not qualified as a legal person; therefore they should carry out activities and develop membership in accordance with the articles of association to which they belongs and the scope of authority of the association.
(2) A social group may not establish a regional branch.
(3) A branch of a social organization may not establish any branch.

55. Cancellation of sports associations. Sports association is one of the common types of legal persons; therefore it has separate legal personality. So it is necessary to carry out the liquidation process when canceled. Reference to the Regulation:

Article 19

The cancellation of associations will be announced after reconfirmation of the authorities in charge and writing off at registering department, when a social organization has any of the following cases:

A. The one has completed the purpose of the Articles of it.

B. The one is self-dissolved.

C. The one is divided or merged.

D. For other reasons.

Article 20

Prior to the registration of cancellation, the social organization shall establish a liquidation group to clear up accounts under the guidance of the competent department and other relevant departments. During the period of liquidation, the social organizations shall not carry out other activities.

§3. Public Safety

56. Generally speaking, "safety" refers to the existence and development of a class of subject that is not under threat.[38] At present, it has not formed a unified definition and cognition for "public safety," however it can be concluded that the public safety is related to the life, the health of non-specific mass and the property of the public and individual.[39] Interpretation of "public" can refer to two points:

(1) It is unspecific, which indicates that the objects involved are not identified.
(2) It is related to the majority, most people or a large number of people, which is a quantitative characteristic.

According to the above-mentioned explanation, the public safety issues of sports associations are often related to organizations of sports competitions and large-scale conferences.

While engaging in the above-mentioned activities, sports associations are still under the system of dual management, which include business guidance of sports departments and safety examination of police departments, excluding departments of civil affairs. At present, one of the relevant laws which is commonly used to regulate these activities is the Regulations on Security Administration of Large-scale Mass Activities. In addition, the Counterterrorism Law of the People's Republic of China which is issued in 2016 also involves the above problems, such as:

Article 34

38. Zhao Hanqing, *Research on Chinese Modern Urban Public Safety Management*, Ph.D. Thesis 9 (Northeast Normal University 2012).
39. Wang Zuofu, *Study on the Criminal Law Practice* 52 (4th ed., China Fangzheng Press 2009).

The entities conducting large-scale activities and managing key targets shall, in accordance with the relevant provisions, implement safety checks for people, goods and vehicles, which enter the large-scale activities places, airports, railway stations, docks, urban rail transit stations, long-distance bus terminals, ports and other key targets. Finding contraband and controlled items should detain and immediately report to the public security organs; finding suspects of illegal acts and crimes should immediately report to the public security organs.

Therefore, while organizing activities, the sports organizations need to fulfill the corresponding security obligations. Specific item of safety obligations should be conducted according to the Regulations on Security Administration of Large-scale Mass Activities:

Article 7

Sponsors shall be specifically responsible for the following security matters:

A. Carrying out the security plans and security responsibility systems for large-scale mass activities, clearly specifying security measures and defining the duties of the security staff, and disseminating the importance of security to large-scale mass activities.

B. Ensuring the safety of temporarily-built facilities and structures, and removing hidden dangers.

C. Installing the necessary equipment for security check in accordance with the requirements of the public security organ in charge of licensing, and conducting security check on the participants of large-scale mass activities, and having the power to refuse entry of the persons who refuse to accept such check.

D. Distributing or selling tickets in keeping with the approved seating capacity of the activity venue and with the designated area.

E. Implementing the emergency rescue measures such as medical treatment and first-aid, fire-fighting and evacuation, and arranging for drills related to such measures.

F. Stopping in a timely manner the acts that interfere with the security of large-scale mass activities, and reporting violations of law or criminal acts to the public security organs as soon as possible upon discovery.

G. Deploying professional security guards and other security staff to meet the needs of security of large-scale mass activities.

H. Providing the necessary guarantee for security of large-scale mass activities.

In addition, the host of large-scale activities should make safety work program, and the content of it shall refer to the Regulation:

Article 6

To hold a large-scale mass activity, the sponsor shall work out a plan for security of such activity.

The security plan for a large-scale mass activity shall include the following:

A. The time, location, content, and way of organization of the activity.

B. The number of security staff, their assignments and identification signs.

C. The fire-fighting measures at the activity venue.

D. The seating capacity of the activity venue and the anticipated number of participants.

E. The fire-fighting measures at the activity venue.

F. The measures for ticket and security check on the participants.

G. The measures for parking of vehicles and for directing their flow.

H. The measures for maintaining order and for directing the flow of participants at the venue.

I. The emergency rescue plan.

So what kind of security program is really "safe"? There is not a unified standard. However, generally, local administrative departments implement security work by the hierarchical management approach according to the actual situation. Such as in the Chinese Football Association Super League, the risk level of security work in Wuhan division has graded levels as "red, orange, and yellow" according to the number of audience; if the number of audience reaches more than 1 million, it is considered to be the red risk level and between 5,000–10,000 people orange risk level, and then yellow risk level is applied to the situation when audiences are small in number and the scene order of a game is relatively stable.

§4. Tax

57. Sports organizations belong to a kind of nonprofit organizations. Therefore, they enjoy a lot of preferential policies in terms of taxation, basically covering all aspects of taxes which the sports associations should pay.

I. Corporate Income Tax

58. According to the relevant laws and regulations, a part of the income of sports associations can enjoy duty-free policy, specifically include:

(1) Financial allocations.
(2) Government funds, capital, additional revenue, approved and charged by the State Council and the Ministry of Finance and drawn into the budget management or financial extra-budgetary funds management.
(3) Administrative fees, approved by the State Council or the people's government at the provincial level (excluding the cities with independent planning) and drawn into the budget management or financial extra-budgetary funds management.
(4) Extra-budgetary funds, which need not be handed over to financial special accounts under approval of the Ministry of Finance.
(5) Special subsidy, which the institution obtains from the competent authorities and the parent unit for development causes.
(6) The income, institutions obtain from after-tax profit of the independent accounting business unit to which they belong.
(7) The funds received from all levels of government.
(8) Membership fees, charged by social groups in accordance with the regulations of provincial civil affairs and financial departments, or above the provincial level.
(9) Donations from all sectors of the society.

Generally, sports associations should apply the following taxes:

(1) Income from the sale of goods.
(2) Income from labor services.
(3) Income from transferring property.
(4) Investment income from dividends, bonuses and other equities.
(5) Interest income.
(6) Rental income.
(7) Income from franchise fees.
(8) Income from donations.
(9) Other income.

The Enterprise Income Tax Law provides the standard rate of 25%, excluding pre-tax deduction of social donations.

II. Business Tax

59. According to the Interim Regulation of the People's Republic of China on Business Tax (2008):

> Article 1
>
> All entities and individuals engaged in the provision of services as prescribed in the present Regulation, the transfer of intangible assets or the sale of immovables within the territory of the People's Republic of China shall be taxpayers of the business tax, and shall pay the business tax in accordance with these Regulations.

In accordance with explanations of the Detailed Rules for the Implementation of the Interim Regulation of the People's Republic of China on Business Tax (2011):

> Article 9
>
> The term "entities" as mentioned in Article 1 of the Regulation refers to enterprises, administrative entities, public institutions, military entities, social groups and other entities.

Therefore, as long as the sports associations engaged in taxable activities, they shall be taxpayer of the business tax. The culture and sports industry are applicable to a tax rate of 3%, of which the sports industry refers to holding a variety of sports competitions or providing places for sports activities for business. Sports associations also enjoy tax concessions in terms of the business tax, mainly including: financial fees and membership fees.

III. Value Added Tax (VAT)

60. According to the Interim Regulation of the People's Republic of China on Value Added Tax (2016):

> Article 1
>
> Entities and individuals engaged in the sale of goods, supply of processing, repair and replacement services, and import of goods within the territory of the People's Republic of China are taxpayers of value added tax (hereinafter referred to as "taxpayers"), and shall pay VAT in accordance with this Regulation.

In accordance with explanations of the Detailed Rules for the Implementation of the Interim Regulation of the People's Republic of China on Value Added Tax(2011):

> Article 9
>
> The term "entity" as mentioned in Article 1 of the Regulation refers to an enterprise, administrative entity, public institution, military entity, social group, etc.

VAT rate is applicable to the general taxpayer. Currently, there are four tax rates: 17%, 13%, 11%, and 6%. The collection rate of the VAT is applicable to small-scale taxpayers and special general taxpayers. Small-scale taxpayers are collected at a rate of 3% uniformly.

IV. Tax Incentives Related to Donation

A. Tax Incentives for Donation of Enterprises

61. According to the Enterprise Income Tax Law of the People's Republic of China:

> Article 9
>
> With regard to an enterprise's disbursements for public welfare donations, the portion that accounts for 12% of the total annual profits or less is allowed to be deducted.

What is more, the amounts of donations for some objects will be deducted in full, including:

(1) Donation for public youth activity places (specifically public service spaces provide science and technology, culture, moral education, patriotism education, Youth Palace of sports activities, Youth Activity Center, and other extracurricular activities for young students).
(2) The China Youth Care Foundation.
(3) China Children and Teenagers' Fund.
(4) The China Foundation for Guangcai Program.
(5) China Education Development Foundation.

B. Tax Incentives for Donation of Individuals

62. For individual donation, including donation of personal and individual for educational and other public welfare institutions, the areas that suffered serious natural disaster and poor areas through social organizations or state organs, the amounts of donations that do not exceed the 30% of income are tax-deductible; any more than the 30% limit shall not be tax deductible.

§5. Dispute Settlement

63. For matters involving public interest, such as the above mentioned, the administrative supervision is the main way for management of sports associations. According to Article 6 of the Law of the People's Republic of China on Administrative Penalty and Article 7 of the Administrative License Law:

Article 6

Citizens, legal persons and other organizations on whom administrative penalty is imposed by administration organs shall have the right to state their cases and the right to defend themselves; those who refuse to accept administrative penalty shall have the right to apply for administrative reconsideration or bring an administrative lawsuit in accordance with law.

Article 7

With regard to an administrative organ's implementation of an administrative license, the citizens, legal person or other institutions shall be entitled to make statements, to defend themselves, to apply for administrative reconsideration or to file an administrative lawsuit in accordance with the law. Where any of their legal rights and interests is impaired because of the administrative organs' unlawful implementation of the administrative license, it shall be entitled to demand compensation in accordance with the law.

Therefore, if the matters are involved in the dispute, the solution is mainly through: administrative reconsideration and administrative lawsuit.

I. Administrative Reconsideration

64. As a legal system to resolve administrative dispute by the administrative organs, administrative reconsideration is referred to a system under which the administrative relative person can request for a review and a decision of the reconsideration departments, when he disagrees on the legitimacy or rationality of an administrative act.[40] In general, several issues of administrative reconsideration should be paid attention to, as follows:

(a) The administrative reconsideration organ in China has the right to accept the administrative application and to make a decision on the specific administrative act. According to the Administrative Reconsideration Law, the determination of the administrative body for reconsideration shall, in general, be divided into four cases:

   (1) For the specific administrative acts of administrative departments at or above the county level, the administrative review organs may be the government at same level, and can also be the competent authorities at the next higher level.
   (2) For the specific administrative acts of the local governments at all levels, the reconsideration organs are the governments at the next higher level. If the government at the next level has a local agency, you can also apply for reconsideration to it.
   (3) For the specific administrative acts of Departments of the State Council and governments of provinces, autonomous regions and municipalities, the reconsideration organs are departments which take specific acts. In case the administrative reconsideration decision is still in dispute, it may bring an administrative lawsuit to the people's court or apply to the State Council for a decision. The decision of the State Council will be final.
   (4) For the specific administrative acts of the vertical management departments, such as the customs, the financial, the tax, the foreign exchange and the state security, the reconsideration organs are the competent departments at the next higher level.

(b) The administrative reconsideration in China is in one-final system, which means if the citizens, legal persons or other organizations refuse to accept decisions of reconsideration, they can only bring administrative lawsuit to the people's court (with the exception of the decision of the State Council).

40. Yang Haikun and Zhu Hengshun, *The Adjustment of the Idea and the Perfection of the System of Administrative Reconsideration – Related to the Important Changes of the Administrative Reconsideration Law and Relevant Laws*, 4 L. Rev. 18 (2014).

(c) In China, the content of administrative reconsideration reviews includes not only the specific administrative acts, but also the abstract administrative ones. According to the Administrative Reconsideration Law:

Article 7

If a citizen, legal person or any other organization considers any of the following provisions, which is the basis of a specific administrative act of an administrative organ, to be illegal, he or it may, when filing an application for administrative reconsideration on a specific administrative act, file an application to the administrative reconsideration organ for reviewing the said provisions:

A. Provisions of departments under the State Council.

B. Provisions of local people's governments at or above the county level and their departments.

C. Provisions of people's governments of towns or townships.

The provisions set forth in the preceding paragraph do not include rules of departments and commissions under the State Council, and local people's governments. Review on rules shall be handled according to relevant laws and administrative regulations.

II. Administrative Lawsuit

65. Administrative litigation is a lawsuit filed by individuals, legal persons or other organizations, when their lawful rights and interests are violated by the administrative bodies and organizations authorized by laws. It is the last and the most powerful means to solve the administrative disputes. According to Chinese law, there are no special restrictions to the plaintiff of communities in the administrative lawsuit, but it is worth describing some special cases of preposition of administrative reconsideration.

Preposition of administrative reconsideration is referred to, when the parties specifically refuse to accept administrative specific acts, they should first choose administrative reconsideration as a remedy, and administrative lawsuit can only be after the reconsideration procedure with which the parties are still not satisfied. In this situation, the court will not accept such administrative proceedings without the prepositive reconsideration procedures.

Generally, for the choice between the administrative reconsideration and administrative lawsuit, it is applied the principle of autonomy for parties, therefore, preposition of administrative reconsideration must be strictly in accordance with separate laws. The cases involved are mainly including:

(1) General reposition of administrative reconsideration. The parties shall apply for a reconsideration of the specific administrative act first, and may bring an administrative lawsuit after it. Such as in the Customs Law:

Article 64

When there are tax disputes with the customs, taxpayer shall pay taxes first, and may apply for administrative reconsideration according to law. If the decision of the reconsideration is still not satisfactory, they may bring a lawsuit to the people's court.

(2) Selective final after reconsideration. The parties can choose lawsuit or adjudication after prepositive reconsideration; however, if they choose adjudication, it will be final. This approach is currently in the Administrative Reconsideration Law:

Article 14

For the specific administrative acts of Departments of the State Council and governments of provinces, autonomous regions and municipalities, the reconsideration organs are departments which take specific acts. In case the administrative reconsideration decision is still in dispute, it may bring an administrative lawsuit to the people's court or apply to the State Council for adjudication. The decision of the State Council will be final.

(3) Final reconsideration. That means the parties can only choose the reconsideration, and the results of the reconsideration is final. Such as in the Exit and Entry Administrative Law:

Article 64

Foreigners dissatisfied with the measure imposed on them in accordance with this Law, such as continued interrogation, detention for investigation, movement restriction or repatriation, may apply for administrative reconsideration in accordance with the law, and the administrative reconsideration decision shall be final.

Where other overseas personnel dissatisfied with the decision of repatriation imposed on them in accordance with this Law apply for administrative reconsideration, the provisions in the preceding paragraph are applicable.

Currently, the disputes related to preposition of reconsideration mainly include:

(1) Infringement on using right and ownership of natural resources.
(2) Disputes on tax.
(3) Decision of audit.
(4) Decision of the Patent Re-examination Board.
(5) Cases of antitrust.
(6) The penalties on price-related violations.

Chapter 3. Private Regulation

66. For the legal person's classification, the traditional civil law theory generally uses the classification of public and private legal person. In private, it is divided into association and incorporated foundation according to the difference of established foundation, and according to the purpose of establishment, divided into the profit-making and the public welfare. Instead of these , the classification of the legal person in civil law theory adopts a different standard in China (Figure 2).

Figure 2 Classification of Legal Person in China

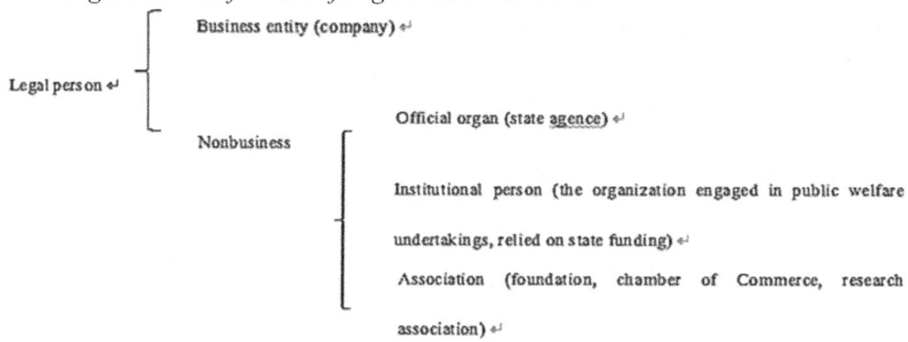

Therefore, the concept of social groups in Chinese theory is not equal with traditional civil laws, which not only includes community but also covers foundation.

§1. The Civil Subject Qualification of Sports Communities

I. General Issues

67. The qualification of the civil subject is also called the capacity of the civil subject, which refers to the ability of the civil subject to enjoy civil rights and assume civil obligations. According to the General Principles of the Civil Law, the civil subjects include three kinds: natural persons, legal persons, and other organizations. Generally speaking, whether a sports social group can have the qualification of civil subject depends on whether it is satisfied to be a legal person. Referring to the General Principles:

Paragraph 2 of Article 50

If according to Law an Institution or Social Organization having the qualifications of a legal person needs not go through the procedures for registering as a legal person, it shall be qualified as a legal person on the day it is established; if according to Law it does need to go through the registration procedures, it shall be qualified as a legal person after being approved and registered.

Therefore, sports associations, which meet the statutory registration conditions, will obtain legal personality to become a civil subject. In addition, according to the Regulation on Registration and Administration of Social Organizations, there are several categories of groups that do not need to pass the registration process:

Paragraph 3 of Article 3

These regulations do not apply to the following organizations:

A. Peoples organizations which participate in the Chinese People's Political Consultative Conference.

B. Organs under the administration of the authorized State Council departments.

C. State organs and groups, enterprises and institutional units, and their internal bodies or groups.

68. The first category is a part of the basic political system in China, which is related to the establishment of China's patriotic united front and the system of multi-party cooperation, and it is protected by the constitution. Therefore, it is not included in the scope of registration groups. For the second category, since the State Council is the unit in charge of the Department of civil affairs, the review of the State Council has completed the substance of administrative supervision in fact, so registration at the CAD is unnecessary. A common feature of these two groups is having stronger publicity than general ones, and accepting a higher level of approval than CADs. The third kind of subjects is not required to register because the areas of activity of it are only limited to the unit and so it does not have the social character in a general sense.

69. Are the three categories of subjects belonging to the scope of the legal person? According to the General Principles mentioned above, the three categories of subjects should belong to legal person of community which does not need to apply for registration, so in accordance with the provisions, as long as having the qualifications of a legal person, the above three categories of subjects would have the qualifications of a legal person since its establishment. This corollary is undoubted when applying to the first two kinds. However, due to lack of social and independent characteristics, the third subject is difficult to be considered a kind of "social group," which makes it no practical significance to discuss whether or not it is a kind of legal person.

70. In addition, looking from the actuality of China, there is a large number of non-governmental sports associations (or "grassroots sports associations") that did not have legal procedures, and did not possess the status of a legal person. To integrate this kind of sports organizations into regulation of the General Principles, they are assigned to the scope of "other organizations" (people-run non-enterprise).

71. To sum up, the sports associations in China exist in two forms. The first is the general sports association, also known as corporate sports association; the second is unincorporated sports community, both of which have the qualification of civil subject. It is a breakthrough for the traditional theory of civil subject to incorporate unincorporated organization into the scope of the civil subject, which is for the needs of the civil procedure and the reality.

II. Establishment Conditions of General Social Groups (Registration Type)

72. For the elements of the establishment of a legal person, it is generally believed that it should have the independent will, independent property, independent lawsuit status and independent responsibility, which is adopted by the civil law in China. According to the General Principles:

Article 37

A legal person shall have the following qualifications:

A. Establishment in accordance with the Law.

B. Possession of the necessary properties or funds.

C. Possession of its own name, organization and premises.

D. Ability to independently bear civil Liability.

73. The provision is the general requirements for establishment of legal person, the corporate sports associations also need to meet the requirements of Articles 10 (*see* "restrictions on freedom of association") and 13 of the Regulation on Registration and Administration of Social Organizations:

Article 13

In any of the following circumstances, the registration authority shall not accept the registration:

A. The purpose and scope of business of the application of a social group for registration are not in conformity with Article 4[41] of this Regulation.

B. For the same or similar business scope within the same administrative region, it is no need to establish the social organization.

C. The initiator and the principal are or have been deprived of political rights of criminal penalties, or do not have full capacity of civil conduct.

D. Frauds in application and preparation.

E. Other circumstances prohibited by laws and administrative regulations.

III. The Civil Subject Restrictions of Unincorporated Sports Community

74. There are two kinds of attitudes about entity law and procedural law subject qualification of the unincorporated corporate:

(1) Because the unincorporated community has been given certain rights from the substantive law, it, of course, has the ability of the parties, and the two main qualifications does not exist separation, which is the view of "not separated" point.
(2) Unincorporated community is not a legal person, nor a civil subject. It does not have right ability. However, the view does not deny that it has the ability of the parties. This is a claim that the unincorporated community's subject qualifications of the entity law and procedural law can be "divided."

For the above point of views, academia mainly support the view of "separation": Though the unincorporated association is different with natural person and legal person for it cannot undertake the responsibility independently, however, it has the corresponding capacity for civil rights and capacity for civil conduct and has the qualification of civil subject. It can be seen from the three main definitions of the unincorporated community:

41. Social organizations must observe the constitution, state laws, regulations and state policy; must not oppose the basic principles of the constitution, harm the unity, security or ethnic harmony of the state, or interests of the state and society, or the lawful interests of other organizations or citizens, or offend social morality. Social organizations may not undertake profit seeking activities.

(1) The so-called unincorporated community is the organization that does not have legal person qualification, but can be engaged in the activity in the name of oneself.[42]
(2) Though unincorporated community does not have personality of group, it is the organization which has "a formal qualification of the civil subject".[43]
(3) Unincorporated community is a subject of civil activities besides the legal person and the natural person.[44]

We agree with the "separation theory".

As previously mentioned, though the unincorporated community is integrated into subjects of civil law, which is for demands of civil procedure and reality, if you think it has full capacity for civil conduct, especially the capacity for civil liability, it is clearly unfair for the other civil parties, which is easy to cause the right abuse.

§2. Civil Liability Issues

I. Corporation Sports Community

75. The legal person is an organization which has been anthropomorphized by law, and has the capacity of civil rights and the capacity for civil conduct, and has the capacity to enjoy civil rights and bear the civil obligations independently. It is an important symbol, whether it can undertake civil liability independently or not, to distinguish between legal persons and other organizations. A legal person has its own independent property, which can be used in its own name to bear civil liability independently. As a type of legal person, the corporate social organization certainly has the ability to independently bear civil liability.

76. Generally speaking, the behavior of a legal person would be identified. Only if implemented in the name of legal person and authorized by decision-making body of the legal person, regardless of whether it is for business and legitimate, the legal person should bear civil liability. On the identification of corporate behavior, the following questions should be explained:

(1) There must be infringement acts and damages of a legal representative or staff to other people, and there are no exemption conditions of law. The Tort Law has strict requirements on the conditions of liability for damages caused by civil tort. Under normal circumstances, the behavior of people to bear the civil liability must be in fault. Therefore, whether the legal person should bear civil liability for the infringement of the legal representative and the staff depends on whether the act meets the conditions for the civil liability led by tort. Therefore, to determine

42. Liang Huixing, *Civil Law* 141–142 (2nd ed., Law Press 2001).
43. Yin Tian, *Study on the Theory and Legislation of Civil Subject* 240 (Law Press 2009).
44. Liu Zhewei, *The Unincorporated Association Qualifications of Civil Subject*, 4 Soc. Sci. in Xinjiang 73 (2005).

whether the legal person shall bear civil liability or not, it shall be based on the specific circumstances of the legal representative or the staff of it.

(2) The result of the damage must be due to the behavior of legal representative or staff. In the law, the behavior of legal representative is regarded as legal person's own. Therefore, the tort of the legal representative in the purview of its authorization is identified as the infringement act of the corporate. Of course, legal person should bear the consequences. Besides, the legal person's business activities also need to be carried out by the staff, that is, the authorized staff would be engaged in business activities in the name of the legal person. Although the status of staff is different from legal representatives, his behavior cannot be regarded as a legal person's own, only an agent's. However, the business activities, which staff involves in, is for the legal person's will to seek benefits. Therefore, for the infringement of staff, the legal person should also bear civil liability.

(3) The infringement of legal representative or staff must occur in business activities. Only if in the process of executing the relevant business activities when the legal representative or the stuff causes damage to others, the responsibility would be borne by the legal person. But if a tort is unrelated to business activities of the corporate or purely implemented personally, the corporate shall not assume civil liability. For example, the stuff goes out in work-time to participate in a fight, causing others to hurt.

In addition, according to the relevant laws, legal person undertakes limited liability for all property, and it has the right of recourse against legal representative and staff in fault.

II. Unincorporated Sports Community

77. Unincorporated sports community does not have legal personality, so it cannot bear civil liability independently like corporation sports community. As Yintian said, "It is far less to say that unincorporated community repays the debt with its 'own' property, than to say that it repays others' (legal person, partnership and initiator or community members) debt with property of 'others'".[45] The General Principles of the Civil Law does not have a clear regulation on civil liability of sports communities, so it can only refer to the provisions on the responsibility of individual partnership:

Article 35

A. A partnership's debts shall be secured with the partners' property in proportion to their respective contributions to the investment or according to the agreement made.

45. Yin Tian, *The Legal Status of Unincorporated Community*, 5 Modern L. Sci. 16 (2003).

B. Partners shall undertake joint Liability for their partnership's debts, except as otherwise stipulated by Law. Any partner who overpays his share of the partnership's debts shall have the right to claim compensation from the other partners.

78. The joint and several liabilities here refer to the joint and several of the members of the unincorporated body. Because that unincorporated sports community lacks legal personality, it should assume unlimited liability with property of all members of it (equivalent to a partner).

79. However, unincorporated sports community still belongs to a class of civil subjects, so the condition under which behavior of its members belonging to the group becomes particularly important:

(1) According to the articles (or agreement) of the association. Unincorporated sports community although does not have the qualifications of a legal person, it still belongs to "a group of persons." Therefore, only the behavior performed in the name of the group (formal condition) and implemented for interests of all members (substantive condition) shall be regarded as the community's. Therefore, it is necessary to refer to the scope of activities ruled by the articles of a association to identify whether the conditions are established.

(2) The duty behavior of unincorporated sports community's responsible person. Referring to the General Principles:

Paragraph 2 of Article 34

The partners may elect a responsible person. All partners shall bear civil Liability for the operational activities of the responsible person and other personnel.

An unincorporated sports community may elect the person in charge, which is carrying out social activities of the plenipotentiary. Responsible person belongs to the "agent" in the law, and the act of agent should belong to the principal. Though the agent is in the name of the group, however, it represents all members in essence. Therefore, if a behavior of responsible person goes beyond the scope of authorization, and does not constitute the apparent agency, the responsibilities should be accepted by the actor himself.

Part II. Sport and Status

Chapter 1. General Issues

80. Sports professionals are the those who are engaged in sports, skills transfer, training and guidance, organization, and management system. The sports professionals include athletes, coaches and referees, sports teachers and administrative staff, etc. Athletes, coaches, and referees are the main body of sports professionals in China.

§1. The Main Types of Sports Professionals

I. Athletes

81. Athletes are the participants of sports competitions, so protecting the rights of the athletes and achieving fairness as well as civilization of the competition is very necessary. *Regulations on Beijing Competitive Sports* (2006) have set the provisions that the players shall abide by. Athletes should abide by the relevant laws, regulations, rules, and comply with the management system of the sports. Athletes shall not use drugs, and they should consciously accept safety check. Besides, they should abide by the management system, and should not affect the normal order of the sports or interfere with the public security. They also should observe social ethics.

II. Coaches

82. Coaches refer to those who cultivate and train sports athletes, and they have the theoretical knowledge of special movement and a higher level of technology, master the advanced teaching and training method. They design, train, guide, and supervise the athlete's mind, body, technique and tactics, and moral character, in order to encourage athletes to improve faster than their original level. In the early 1970s in the United States (US), coach's technology is a new and effective management technology which originated from daily life and conversations, sports psychology and pedagogy, and can help gain insight into itself, maximize individual potential, effectively stimulate the team and bring the power of the whole into full play, so as to improve the productivity of the enterprises. Through a series of directional and strategic management, coaches can gain insight into the mental models of the athletes, excavate potential inward and find possibilities outward, effectively reaching the goal.

III. Referees

83. According to competition rules, the referee is the person who evaluates athletes' (team) performance, results, and rankings. The referee is not only a "law enforcement" in the competition, but also the organizer and leader, whose level directly affects athletes technical and tactical performance as well as the effect of the game.

84. The referee plays an important role in sports competitions, so it is important to guarantee the fairness of a game by regulating a referee's behavior. For example, *The Implementation of Tianjin Sports Competition Rules for Referee Registration*, provides the referee's scope of registration, the procedure, authority and date, fee of registration, etc.

§2. Professionals' Specification of Sports in China

85. The Professionals' specification of sports in China is composed of sports industry norms and legal norms.

86. The Professionals' specification of sports in China is the combination of international sports norms and China Sports Federation specification. For sports' professionals, there are two main specifications: the first one refers to the rules and regulations made by the International Olympic committee (IOC), national Olympic committee, and International Sports Federation.

87. The second one is the rules and regulations formulated by Chinese Olympic Committee (COC), the Chinese Sports Federation and the national sport organization. As these organizations belong to sports social groups and not organs of state power and government agencies, they cannot refer to the laws and regulations, and do not belong to the legal category.[46]

88. The types of sports law include regulation, rules, measures, and implementing details. Sports legislative system is the system and structure that formed by the division of legislative purview. Chinese sports legislative system is the unitary two-stage legislative system of multiple hierarchy. Unity means only one nationwide unitized system and integrative legislation, no other one existing. Two-stage means legislative system consists of central government and local governments. In multiple hierarchies, legislative system can be divided into several hierarchies and categories.

89. Normative document, drafted and released by NPC and standing committee for whole sports work, are called sports law. Sport administrative law drafted or approved by the State Council focuses on certain respect of sports administrative work. Measures are a kind of relatively concrete documents of specific sports administrative work. Implementing details are definite arrangements, explanation, and complementariness for implementing national sports' related law, administrative regulations or administrative rules and regulations.

46. Zhang Houfu, *Sport Jurisprudence* 33–34 (People's Sports Press 2001).

90. The State Council of the PRC and the department of administrative management under the State Council have drawn up a series of rules and regulations, for example, *The Rules of Athletes, the Grading Systems of Athletes, the Codes of Excellent Sport Teams*, for the purpose of strengthening sports teams, raising political and cultural ability of athletes, climbing to the peak of sports performance, achieving honor and reputation for the country.

Chapter 2. Public Regulation

§1. Legal Status

91. China manages the sports professionals through the registration system. In other words, the Chinese sports practitioners gain the sports qualification by registering, which has corresponding legal status.

I. The Registration and Exchange of Athletes

92. Based on Article 29 of *Law of the People's Republic of China on Physical Culture and Sports*, "The national sports association of an individual sport shall manage the registration for athletes. In accordance with the regulations of the administrative department for physical culture and sports under the State Council, a registered athlete may participate in relevant sports competitions and flow from one team to another." On this basis, on August 11, 2003, General Administration of Sport of china issued *The Approach of National Athletes' Registration and Communication Management (on trial)*. The content is as follows.

93. The registration and the exchange of the athletes should be in line with the principle of voluntariness, openness, legality, and order. Registration unit shall provide registration service for athletes within twelve months from the date when the agreement of representative qualification is signed. Beyond the time limit, the agreement representative qualification will be invalid. Provinces, autonomous regions and municipalities directly under the central government, Xinjiang Production and Construction Corps, PLA, sports association of the industry, the participating units of the game of national adolescents and adults, which after approval and recognition from General Administration of Sport of China, the National Association of an Individual Sport or Sports Management Center, becomes a registration qualification units (except Hong Kong and Macao Special Administrative Region). The time limit of representative for agreement that be signed between registered unit and athletes is about two to nine years. The termination date of the agreement of representation for qualifications signed between legal guardians and athletes' registered units shall not be more than sixteen years. As the representation for qualifications protocol expires, the players enjoy the priority of registration.

94. It called for the exchange of athletes: athletes' spa provinces, autonomous regions and municipalities, and sports guilds change their registered institutions. The athletes' exchange should adhere to the principle of voluntariness, mutual benefit, openness, fairness, legality, and order. The exchange of athletes is that the athletes should be registered by national association of sport management center in the General Administration of Sport of China. The exchange of the athletes does not conduct until their agreement with original registered institutions has expired or been terminated. The athletes who belong to the qualified institutions under provinces, autonomous regions, and municipalities have the right to alternate spanning provinces, autonomous regions, municipalities, and sports guilds. It is after two years that the athletes who have regularly dealt with the retired formalities can sign a new agreement with another institution. Meanwhile, they do not pay for the original registered institutions for exchange any longer. During that period, the original registered institutions can agree to retired athletes participating in games representing other institutions, and there are no restrictions for this.

95. In accordance with the magnitude of the case, the athletes, who have signed agreements with above two qualified registration departments in the same period, would be disqualified for one to four years' nationwide competitions correspondingly. For those departments who delay or hinder the athletes' normal communication through any reasons or methods, or who carry on the athletes' exchange improperly by any illegal ways, the General Administration of Sport of China will circulate a notice of criticism, and even disqualify their participation in nationwide individual sports or comprehensive sports competitions.

II. The Referee's Registration

96. The provision of Article 24 in Chapter 4 of *The Approach of Referee's Management in Sports Competition* is that the referees at all levels, who participate in conducting work in national sports competition, must have registration certificates. If the referees without the approval of the unit register for the second time in a row, their technical grade title will be automatically canceled and referees certificate will be invalid. The approval authorities of the referees at all levels must register for the referees' approval every two years, and honorary referees may not be registered. The registration period for the referee of each project is from December 1 every even-number year to February 5 of the next year. After the approval of the administrative department for physical culture and sports under the State Council, the National Association of an Individual Sport shall separately determine the referee's registration period according to characteristics of the project.

97. Primary referees should be registered by physical cultural administrative department at the provincial level or authorized unit of the administrative department for physical culture and sports under the State Council of the PRC, and it will be submitted to the National Association of an Individual Sport for the record. Secondary and tertiary referees should be registered by local, county physical cultural administrative department, and it will be submitted to the provincial SADs for the record. The referees of the level of two and three must register at sports administration department all over the county and report for the provincial sports' administration department. Referees in any of the following circumstances shall be suspended once, such as the referees who are fined by the division or the unit of examination and approval, or whose inspection is unqualified, or referees do not work or attend the courses in two years.

§2. Basic Rights and Obligations

I. Athletes' Rights and Obligations

98. The Athletes' rights refer to the rights prescribed by the Constitution and the law. That is to say, the athletes should realize the interests of the material benefit and spiritual power in the form of act or omission on the basis of their legal status in social life and competitive sports. Therefore, the athletes' rights can be divided into two parts: one is the basic right endowed by the Constitution and the law directly. That is, as an ordinary citizen an athlete should enjoy basic human rights; the other is the professional rights that should be enjoyed by the professionals who fulfill the special training and responsibility of competition, which is the basic right of evolution and extension in the competitive sports industry.[47]

A. *The Athletes' Rights*

99.

(1) The right of equal competition

Competitive sports are the competition activities. It provide wonderful events for public, which is not only the foundation of the survival and development of professional sports but also owns its huge charm; and the basis of sports competitions is derived from fair competition. Therefore, the fair competition becomee

(2) The right of life and health

The right of life and health is the foundation to ensure the life support and security of a natural person. As the basic human right, the right of life and health is protected by international law and domestic law. Article 98 of GENERAL PRINCIPLES OF THE CIVIL LAW OF THE PEOPLE S REPUBLIC OF CHINA describes as follows: the citizens shall enjoy the right of life and health. The right of life and health has special significance for the athletes, which is directly related to the athlete's life and career life of athletes in the future etc. It is the basic requirements that the athletes should enjoy in the player's life and career development.

(3) The right of labor remuneration

47. Dong Xiaolong and Guo Chunling, *Sports Law* 76 (Law Press 2006).

The right of labor remuneration is the athletes' rights based on the labor contract that athletes should have remuneration in accordance with the law.

The right of labor remuneration is the core of labor rights, which is not only the strong life safeguard of workers and their families, but also the recognition and evaluation of the society for their labor. It is one of the most basic rights of a laborer in economic rights by "CONSTITUTION OF THE PEOPLE'S REPUBLIC OF CHINA." The labor remuneration of athletes is the main source of athletes and their family life.

(4) The right to education

Citizens shall enjoy the right to the education, and it refers that the citizens have the right to learn culture and scientific knowledge in schools and institutions of various types in state and society. The right to education is a basic rights of citizens endowed by "CONSTITUTION OF THE PEOPLE'S REPUBLIC OF CHINA," and it mainly includes the equal access to education, accepting education process of integrity, comprehensive education and continuing education, etc.

(5) The right to information, defense, hearing and appeal

Any decision involving the vital interests of the athletes, sports administrative institutions should ensure that the athletes have the basic procedural rights, such as the right to information, defense, hearing and appeal.

(6) The right of registration

Registration is the act that the unit of competition submits basic information of athletes to designated department of registration according to the provisions of the relevant documents, in order to meet the demands of management of General Administration of Sport of China and the individual sports associations. Registration is a prerequisite that the players have to meet. It violates the players' registration rights if there is any unreasonable behavior or unequal conditions on athletes' registration. Typical cases are: requiring payment of deposit and signing the unequal contracts, etc.

(7) The rights of free transfer

The transfer of players refers to the athletes flow from the original competition unit to another unit after a certain program. At present, it is very difficult to achieve transfer freely in the field in competitive sports in our country, and some competition unit adopts many means, such as wild speculations, threat and intimidation, to prevent players from having the idea of transferring, imposed additional terms of renewal right of priority in the contract of athletes, etc.

(8) The right of disability health insurance

It is full of severe competition and intense physical confrontation at modern competitive sports, and the phenomenon that athletes are injured and even suffer from damage with long period of high intensity, high load training and competition status is very common. The injuries in sports have a high incidence, universality, concealment, delay, etc. According to statistics, more than 70% athletes in our country have disability in different degree, disability rate and heavy disability rate is close to 30% and many injuries will appear after the athlete retires.

B. The Athletes' Obligations

100. Athletes should undertake the following obligations:

(1) Love sports, bravely peak in competitive sports, win honor for our country.
(2) Train hard, respect coaches, complete the training mission carefully.
(3) Comply with competition rules, obey the referee, respect opponents, respect the audience.
(4) Strengthen the learning, and constantly improve their own quality. Athletes are the main practitioners of competitive sports, and they are the creators, performers and communicators with truth, goodness and beauty, and they should become the main concern of social public and the model for young people to imitate.
(5) Observe the relevant code of conduct and the law, which is the duty for every citizen.
(6) Serve the society, guide and improve the work of social sports.
(7) When taking part in the competition abroad, the excellent athletes should abide by the laws of the host country and our country, safeguard the dignity and rights and interests of our country and comply with the relevant provisions of the international sports organization.

II. The Coaches' Rights and Obligations

101. The coach's rights include:

(1) The coaches have the nomination right for recruiting and assigning athletes.

(2) The coaches have the command right of training and competition.
(3) The coaches have the rights of gaining material to meet the need of training, competition and labor protection.
(4) The coaches have the right to accept the training education.
(5) The coaches have the right to apply for corresponding positions and titles in accordance with the relevant provisions.
(6) The coaches have the right to receive all kinds of spiritual and material rewards for their training, competition, research results.
(7) The coaches have the rights to take part in democratic management.
(8) The coaches have the right to rest for labor.

The coaches' obligations include:

(1) The coaches have the duty to complete relevant training and competition.
(2) The coaches should prepare the teaching training programs and plans for the team according to the law of sports training and the characteristics of the project.
(3) The coaches should study business, use multi-disciplinary knowledge to guide the training and make efforts to improve the level of scientific training.
(4) The coaches should be concerned about the cultural learning of athletes, help the athletes with ideological and political work, mobilize the athletes' enthusiasm at work, give full play to the wisdom of athletes, train the consciousness and guide the athletes to observe the rules and regulations and set up a good atmosphere.
(5) The coaches should actively cooperate with the team doctor athletes in medical supervision and injury prevention, timely find out the reasons and the responsibility for the injury in the training and competition during sports injury accident.
(6) The coaches should respect each other, the referee, and the audience and obligate duty of management.
(7) The coaches should learn from each other, help each other and obligate the duty of solidarity and collaboration between the coaches.
(8) The coaches should consciously abide by national laws, rules and regulations of General Administration of Sport of China and protect the country's image, honor, and interests.

III. The Rights and Obligations of Referee

102. The referee's rights include:

(1) Take part in national referee work of various competitions.
(2) Take part in the referee's learning and training organized by the related departments.
(3) Supervise the system of the referee organization to perform at the corresponding level.
(4) Accept the labor remuneration that is paid by the sports contest organizers.
(5) Accuse the unhealthy phenomenon in the referee team of this project.
(6) The referee have the right to make complaints for referee departments to the next higher level and to make technical punishment at the corresponding level.

Judges in various levels shall undertake the following obligations:

(1) Foster and stick to good professional morality, fair law enforcement in the competition work.
(2) Work on the project rules and judging method.
(3) Train and guide the referees under different levels.
(4) Undertake the tasks of examination and approval assigned by examination and approval authority and act as a referee in next level sports.
(5) Carry out the investigation of enforcement of referees along with the referee Organization.

§3. Hierarchy

103. Article 30 of *Law of the PRC on Physical Culture and Sports* describes as follows: "The State practices a skill-grading system for athletes and referees, and a grading system of professional and technical titles for coaches." According to this law, General Administration of Sport of China promulgates *The System of Technical Grade of Athletes*, *The Grades System of Coaches' Post in Sports* and *The Measures for the Management of Sports' Referees (on trial).* The content is as follows.

I. The Technical Level of Athletes

104. It implements the examination and approval system for the technical level of athletes in china. On January 10, 2014, the first director's office meeting of General Administration of Sport of China promulgated *System of Technical Grade of Athletes*, namely the eighteen orders of General Administration of Sport of China. Chinese athletes' ranking titles include: world-class athletes, master sportsmen, first-class athletes, second-class athletes, and third-class athletes. The management of level of ranking titles practices graded examination and approval, hierarchical authorization. According to the authorization of the General Administration of Sport of China, the departments, such as the provincial sports' administration department, General Administration of Sport in the Xinjiang Production and Construction Corps, the Military physical Training Authority in Military Training Department of People's Liberation Army General Staff Department, the Culture and Sports Bureau in the propaganda department of People's Liberation Army General Political Department, etc., have the right to approve first-class athlete, second-class athletes and third-class athletes. According to actual condition, provincial administrative department of sports can grant the approval rights of second-class athletes and third-class athletes to the municipal administrative department for physical culture and sports within their respective administrative areas, and approval authority for third-class athletes can also be given to the administrative department of county level within their respective administrative areas.[48]

48. The System of Technical Grade of Athletes of January 10, 2004.

II. Technical Level of the Coaches

105. The degree of coaches can be divided into: the third-level coaches, the second-level coaches, the first-level coaches, the senior coaches, and the national level coaches. The first two of them belong to the primary post, the middle one is an intermediate post, and the last two are advanced.

III. The Referee's Grade of Specialized Technical Post

106. Based on the degree and professional level of referees, the sport administrative department under the State Council and the physical culture and sport administrative departments examine and endorse, register, and manage at different grades of the referees. The National Sports Associations for Individual Sport authorized by the sport administrative department under the State Council take charge of the examination and register of the referee above state level on relevant sports programs. The local sport administrative departments at different levels take charge of the assessment and register of referee within their administrative area. Article 8 of Chapter 3 of *Measures for the Management of Referee in the Sports Competition (on trial)* in China describes as follows:

> The hierarchy of referees can be divided into international level, national level, the first level, the second level, the third level and honorable referees. The sport administrative departments at the country level examine and approve the third-level referee, the local and municipal people's government to the second-level referee, the province to the first-level, the sport administrative department under the State Council to the national referee, the International Sports Associations for Individual Sport to the international level. The referees' approval departments at different levels must hold a promotion test at least every two years. The punishment for referees can be divided into: warning, disqualification for the competition, stopping the referee work for two years, cancellation for grading titles and ceasing the referee work for lifelong time. The referees will be punished when offering or accepting bribes and denial of justice, or failure to judge in the significant match that causes bad effect. If someone is in violation of criminal law or gets criminal penalty, the professional title would be canceled and the referee work must be stopped for the lifetime.

§4. Labor Market Regulation

107. The Chinese government attaches great importance to the employment work of sports professionals. Article 28 in *Law of the People's Republic of China on Physical Culture and Sports* (1995) states: "The State grants preferential treatment to outstanding athletes in their employment and enrollment for schools."

108. As for the placement of athletes, on the one hand, the personnel departments of government at all levels and sport administrative departments can possibly arrange them to be coaches, managers, and workers inside the sport system; on the other hand, they may get in touch with the state organs, public institutions, state-owned business, collectively owned enterprises and schools, etc. and make them to be the staffs in the union, office workers or teachers, etc. Some can be placed at the same position as the officers and civil cadres transferred to civilian work.

109. In order to adapt to the needs of establishing the socialist market economy and the development of undertakings of physical culture and sports, to strengthen the construction of sports teams and solve problems of athletes, to arouse the enthusiasm of athletes dedicated to the undertakings of physical culture and sports and to promote the improvement of technical level, on September 29, 2002, Central People's Government of the PRC issued *The Opinion of Further Work to the Settlement of Employment for Retired Athletes* on the basis of the relevant provisions of *The Labor Law of the People's Republic of China* and *Law of the People's Republic of China on Physical Culture and Sports*. The regulations stipulate athletes' employment from four aspects: first, the local people's governments at various levels and the relevant departments should attach great importance to the employment of retired athletes; second, the Chinese government should set up and improve social security system and employment training system of the athlete; third, The Chinese government create conditions to widen the channel of the job and encourage retired athletes to choose their work independently and actively; fourth, strengthen cultural education for athletes, make themselves constantly improve their own quality, and provide a basis for employment in school.

§5. Social Security

110. Athletes are important to the development of sports enterprise in our country, which strengthens athletes' culture education. Increasing athletes' social security earnestly is of great significance to comprehensive, harmonious, and sustainable development of sports undertakings.

The center of the social security for sports professionals' athletes in Chinese mainly focuses on three aspects: first, the culture and education; second, job security; third, the sports awards.

I. The Cultural Education

111. On March 30, 2010, Central People's Government of the PRC issued *The Guidance of Further Strengthening Culture Education and Guidance of Security Work of the Athletes*. This Article 1 points out: local governments at all levels must attach great importance to the integration work of resource of the administrative department for physical culture and sports and the administrative department of education during training stages of reserve personnel in competitive sports, and establish appropriate mechanisms for leadership. The administrative department for physical culture and sports and the administrative department of education at all levels should build the joint conference systems of culture education and supervision system for the athlete and give priority to the administrative department for physical culture and sports, which forms the management system and operational mechanism of backup in competitive sports in which the administrative department of sports and education are responsible for themselves.

112. According to *Compulsory Education Law of the People's Republic of China*, athletes should accept nine-year compulsory education. Outstanding athletes under 30-year old, the winners those who are placed in front three of individual sport and who are the leading players in front three of group events, as well as the world record holder in the Olympics, the World Cup, or the World Championships, will be free of the National Entrance Examinations of Universities and Colleges, but they must pass the required testing organized by universities and colleges, after the consultation meeting during General Administration of Sport of China, State Education Commission, and relevant colleges and universities.

II. Job Security

113. Article 18 in *The Guidance of Further Strengthening Culture Education and Guidance of Security Work of the Athlete* states that: the public employment service agencies at all levels should actively provide the services of employment and career guidance for athletes. The social security administration departments of human resources at all levels and the administrative department for physical culture and sports should actively create conditions for retired athletes to find jobs, broaden employment channels, guide and support the training and learning for retired athletes to enter colleges and universities and all kinds of vocational school, constantly improve the comprehensive quality and employment ability, and help them achieve career changes.

114. Also, the retired athletes can obtain retirement fee or economic compensation of profession according to the relevant provisions. According to the factors such as the development level of local economic and price index, the local government should set up dynamic adjustment mechanism of the athletes' economic compensation standard, and adjust the standard of economic compensation. According to the regulation, the athletes have free choice and can enjoy corresponding support policy of employment. The retired athletes who want self-employment should be given policy support.

III. Sports Awards

115. Sports administrative reward means government administrative departments give material and psychological encouragement to the persons and groups who have done notable contribution for the country according to the legal term. The purpose of sports administrative reward is honoring the advanced and encouraging the backward which can arouse the enthusiasm and creativity for the socialist cultural and ethical progress.

The principles of sports administrative reward: (a) material and mental reward combined; (b) legal standard and seeking the truth from the fact; (c) the reward matching the behavior; (d) fairness and equality.

The contents of sports administrative reward. Rewards give person certain rights and interests by encouraging actions. According to the related law, the reward content consists of three parts:

(1) Rights and interests in the mental respect. The rewarded people gain legal glory acknowledged by country and society, such as championship and member of Sports Civilization Advanced Unit.
(2) Rights and interest in the material respect. People gain amount of reward money, prize, and promotion to certain salary.
(3) Rights and interest in the aspect of post and professional titles. The rewarded persons are promoted to certain post and get certain professional titles.

Reward forms. Based on different situation, the legal norms have different rules, concluded as following:

(1) Circulated praise.
(2) Contributions.
(3) Raised Salary.
(4) Job promotion.
(5) Commendation.
(6) Material rewarding.
(7) Honorary title.

Reward procedure. According to the existing law and regulation, the encouraging procedures are as following:

(1) Nomination.
(2) Approval.
(3) Announcement.
(4) Prize-awarding.
(5) Keeping in the archives.[49]

§6. Dispute Settlement

I. General Situation

116. On May 25, 1999, China General Administration of Sport released the no. 2 decree—*Regulations for Sports Rules Program*, which is a good beginning to provide basis for establishing our sports laws. On August 20, 2005, *Regulations of Programming Rules for General Administration of Sport* were released. Although the promulgating behaviors of General Administration of Sport shows it attaches importance to the procedures of law making, no sports procedural law has been legislated yet.

49. Zhang Houfu, *Sport Jurisprudence* 50–52 (People's Sports Press 2001).

117. There may appear deviations when the sports administrative authorities (including different kinds of associations) execute their administrative power, for there is no law about sports administrative procedures. For this reason, it is hard to rationally distribute either the procedural or the substantive rights and obligations between the parties.[50]

118. In any department law, strict procedural law is the assurance of the implement of the department law. For example, Article 49 of *Law of the PRC on Physical Culture and Sports* states that: "Whoever commits fraud or other acts violating the discipline or sports rules in competitive sports shall be punished by the relevant public sports organization in accordance with the provisions of its articles of association." This kind of punishment would have great effect on athletes or sports clubs, because it may even terminate their sports career (e.g., the punishment of taking doping is the life ban). So, it is necessary to set strict procedures for disciplinary punishment. Although this kind of procedure cannot be as strict as judicial procedure, it should guarantee the rights of those who are punished.

119. Article 33 of *Law of the PRC on Physical Culture and Sports* states that: "Disputes arising in competitive sports activities shall be mediated and arbitrated by sports arbitration institutions. Measures for the establishment of sports arbitration institutions and the scope of arbitration shall be prescribed separately by the State Council." But this article did not give rise to unified sports arbitration institutions. More than ten years has passed, the State Council still has not released *the Regulations for Sports Arbitration*, and we believe that, we will not set up sports arbitration system without sports arbitration procedure. But, we still have a long way to go to set up the sports arbitration system of our country; we need to broadly considerate the sports procedural regulations for the establishment of the sports arbitration system.[51]

120. Competitive sports litigation and relief mechanism is the whole judicial system provided for the parties in the sports disputes. Competitive sports disputes litigation and relief is actually a kind of mechanism provided for the parties in the legal dispute in the sports, from which they can gain equal access to judicial relief. It should be emphasized that litigation have the right to intervene, can intervene, rather than must, or totally be involved.

II. The Status of China's Athletics Litigation Relief Mechanism

A. The Legal Basis Is Not Clear

121. At present, in China, the *Law of the People's Republic of China on Physical Culture and Sports* is the only one that formulated law on the sports dispute resolution and its provisions for content-based principle. Due to lack of specific operation, it will not directly function as a sports intervention or judicial review basis; the administrative regulations about sports is a relatively large number, many of which also involves

50. Luo Jiasi, *Reflections on Programming Legal Standard of Sports*, 3 J. Wuhan Inst. Physical Educ. (2000).

51. Lu Pan and Kong Yunlong, *Construction of the Procedure Our Country's Sports Arbitration,* 1 J. Anhui Agric. U. (social sciences version) (2010).

sports executive and industry organizations to exercise public power, but for judicial intervention, there are almost no other external means of settlement provisions. There are a relatively large number of departmental rules and local regulations, but all of them lack relevant relationship, and because they only have "light" effect, they cannot serve as strong support for judicial intervention; meanwhile, some articles of association of sports industry have articles of association for the industry within the field of dispute resolution in different types of treatment, and also the requirements are not uniform, and incomplete, some of which even are contrary to the provisions of laws and regulations.

B. The Focus of Relief Is Not Prominent

122. Due to the limitation of "exhaustion of internal remedies" principle, in practice, many sports have been treated before submitted to the court. If we do not highlight that the sports litigation should be based on relief program, but instead conduct the full trial blindly, not only can the dispute be solved, but also the valuable judicial resources will be wasted. However, sports disputes cannot find a good balance between the self-discipline and the heteronomy.

C. The Trial Is Not Professional

123. Sports disputes have technical and highly professional characteristic. If the parties are those whose interests are affected by these professional issues, the procedural fairness will not be achieved. To solve this problem, some countries have begun to set up sports court, and some of them have even set up separate sports courts to resolve such disputes. China's existing sports court cases shall be heard by ordinary civil tribunals, administrative tribunals, criminal courts. However, the setup of the court staff does not meet the general requirements of professional review. Because many judges do not have the relevant knowledge of sports, even though the case is judged fairly, it often gives people a feeling of lack of authority. This is the important reason why a lot of people refuse to judicial intervention.

D. The Delay of the Trial Is Prominent

124. In China, the court proceedings are often not fast enough, unable to solve some immediate demands of sports disputes, which can be perfected through the improvement of judicial reforms. But all this does not completely solve the people's question to the sports litigation relief mechanism. Sports parties think that as judicial protection to their rights is not timely, they have no desire for the legal counsel of their dispute.[52]

52. Xu Huaiguang, *Sports Relief Mechanism of a Dispute,* excellent master degree paper, 6 (2008).

III. The Ideas of Perfecting the Existing Sports Litigation Settlement Mechanism

125. Through the analysis above, it is not difficult to find, two main reasons affecting the litigation: first, the requirements of sports disputes own characteristics; second, the judicial system. As current sports litigation settlement mechanisms are inadequate, we should take the right measures and make improvements in the following areas. First, make the range and type of sports litigation disputes clear; second, we should set up the principles "sports disputes exhausting internal remedies;" third, setting up sports tribunal.

Chapter 3. Sports Industry Standards

§1. The Management of Sports Professionals

126. The Chinese athletic associations have the right of management of the sports professionals. There are mainly three ways: first, legal authorization. Article 29 of *Law of the PRC on Physical Culture and Sports* stipulates: the National Sports Association of An Individual Sport shall manage the registration of athletes of the sport activity. An athlete that has been registered may, in accordance with the regulations of the administrative department for physical culture and sports under the State Council, participate in relevant sports competitions and flow from one team to another; second, the delegate. Article 3 of Chapter 1 of *Measures for the Management of Referee in the Sports Competition (on trial)* in China describes as follows: the National Association of An Individual Sport authorizes the administrative department for physical culture and sports under the state council to assess and register the referees above referee at the national level. Article 4 describes as follows: the National Association of An Individual Sport establishes the referee commission. Under the leadership of each individual sport association, the referee commission study, research, and accurately grasp the international rules, and it is responsible for the training and management of the referees; third, the way of contract. The relations between the members of the sports and associations can be seen as a kind of contractual relationship, and the sports associations can obtain the right of management through related contract.

127. Its main responsibilities include: formulating, managing and organizing the implementation of the sports competition system, plans, procedures, and magistrates, and examining national competition rules validation and athletic performance; carrying out international contact and technological exchange, proposing the sports' internationals program, guiding the organization and training in international team competition, and the approval of holding an international competition, implementing the athletes, referees technical level system in the sport, and training and assessing high level coaches and referees; and organizing the research and publication of professional books and so on.

128. The ways to manage sports professionals mainly are through supervision and management, disciplinary process and dispute resolution.

§2. The Way of Management

I The Regulation of Sports Professionals

129. The main content of the regulation is as follows: first, the registration. Just as Article 34 of *Management Regulations of Registration of Football Association in China (2007)* stipulates, all personnel who are engaged in or prepare to work in the football coaches must be registered. For the football coaches who lead the team of

Chinese football association and the members association must obey *The Coaching Qualification Certificate of Coaches of the Chinese Football Association* (hereinafter referred to as "certificate"), issued by the Chinese football association. The game monitors will check certificate of the coaches at home and abroad before every game. All coaches without "certificate" are not allowed to lead game. Article 43 stipulates: athletes who participates in the football game of Chinese football association and the member association must obey *The Registration Certificate of Transfer, Registration and Qualification for Participating in Competition* (hereinafter referred to as "the registration certificate"). The registration certificate is issued by the Chinese football association or association. Article 49 stipulates: national referees that the Chinese Football Association has approved, and international referees and assistant referees that the Chinese Football Association has recommended and FIFA has approved, should be registered in accordance with the appropriate procedures; second, training. The paragraph 5 in Article 7 of *Constitution of the Chinese Football Association (2005)* stipulates: it is responsible for organizing the training of the coaches and referees and member associations; third, the inspection. As Article 9 of *Referee's Management Approach of Basketball Association in China* prescribes that the referee commission of the Chinese Basketball Association (CBA) is a special committee under the CBA, and it is responsible for the management of the national basketball referees, and the training, examination and approval, management and supervision of the national referees above the state-level referees.

II. The Deregulation Treatment

130. The Individual Sport Association in China owns the power of punishment. Article 8 of *Rules of discipline of the Chinese Football Association* stipulates that the illegal behavior in the Chinese soccer association shall be performed by disciplinary committee in the Chinese football association. Article 13 stipulate that the main types of penalties includes warning (yellow), sending off (red card), suspension, being prohibited from entering the athletes lounge or bench, being prohibited from entering the stadium (hall) and being prohibited to take part in any activities related to football, etc.

The procedure of sports discipline, is also called inner resolution procedure for sports clubs. It is the reflection of self-discipline. It is within the scope of administrative penalty. As the sports associations had less administrative power as time passed by, the subject range was extended.

131. Sports punishment means that the authorities or individuals who have the power according to the law or regulations make the punishing decision to those who has done undue behavior in sports games or those who take sports as career has done undue behaviors. The author makes this demarcation for the reason that the punishment related to sports contains not only things but also people. The punishment on things means that the relevant authorities (e.g., state judicial organ, sports organizations or judges) punish those undue behaviors, such as bribery, taking doping, and technical foul and so on; punishment on people means that in order to maintain the image of sports, sports organizations punish those who take sports as career has done undue behaviors out of the games, such as excessive drinking, brawling and fighting, and other behaviors irrelevant to sports.[53]

III. The Dispute Settlement

132. The fractions in the sports club always occur in the application of the club rules which are currently in effect. The relationship between the sports club and their members is sports administrative relationship, and the fractions always are dealt with the inner dispute settlement procedures. The inner administrative disputes take place in the process of applying club rules based on the autonomous right of sports club, including: (1) the sports disputes about qualification problem; (2) the disputes aroused by refusing to obey disciplinary punishment; (3) the disputes aroused by certain behavior and decision (not including the punishments). However, the inner dispute settlement system in the sports club must be based upon the upstanding system construction to ensure the impartiality of its judgment, which includes the necessary procedure, giving the athletes right to attorney. In a word, the establishing and consummating of inner dispute settlement procedures of the sports club is a major task of the sports industry in our country.

A. The Imperfections of Our Sports Disciplines

133. Recent years, the disputes aroused by the dissatisfaction with the sports disciplines have increased obviously, which are mainly about the proliferation of professional sports and Olympic events (stimulants). The reasons why the disputes appear with a high frequency are: (1) pluralistic interests; (2) the backwardness of our sports management mechanism, and our sports management mechanism are trailed by the reality in the aspect of idea, way of act, and the system construction; (3) the negative effect brought by the commercialization; (4) the absence of the consummate procedural safeguard and relief procedure.

134. Our country's sports clubs acquire the monopolistic power while lacks effective external supervision and internal control, which causes the members' misidentification to the club, and the club does not has the authority and cohesive force. As for the sports disciplines, due to the lack of the control to the power, the unbalance between the clubs' power and the counterpart's right, and the system construction lacking attention of the people, and the low sports clubs' enforcement quality, the sports disciplines have many problems. For example, the basis of Chinese Football Association rejecting the jurisdiction's intervention violates legal regulations, which has caused the last punishment to violate the principle of procedural justice, harmed the party's interest, aroused the turbulence of football world, and affected the development of our country's professional sport.

53. Han Yong, *The Study on Sports Disciplinary Punishment*, excellent doctor degree paper, 6 (2006).

B. The Consummation of Sports Disciplines

135. We should consummate our country's sports disciplines and supply judicial approaches. The settlement of professional sports in our country, currently, always depends on the interest parties' reconciliation of their own accord and the sports club "inner settlement or administration department" intercession and adjudication. As the specialty and technicality of sports disputes, people seldom appeal to the court. Even in this case, the court is unwilling to hear the case.

136. First, we should unify the inner dispute-settling mechanism and procedures of national sports club, so that it can be connected to the sports arbitration system effectively. Second, we should organize pluralistic disputes remedies system. On the one hand, we should set up our country's sports arbitration agency, and according to the rules about the athletic sports' intercession and adjudication in *The Law of Physical Culture and Sports and* we should draw up the administration regulations of sport arbitration which conforms to sports socialization and institutionalize, coordinating with international conventions, settling disputes speedily, concisely, conveniently and economically. On the other hand, we should alter the *Law of Physical Culture and Sports.* Stipulating the punishments which violated the procedural justice can receive judicial review in the professional sports.

Especially, we should quickly establish our country's sports arbitration agency, so that it can consummate and perfect our professional sports disciplines, ensure sports disciplines' procedural justice and preserve the people legal interests.[54]

54. Liu Su & Tang Weidong, *The Study on the Procedural Justice of Sports Disciplines in the American Four Balls Professional Alliance – The Inspiration to Consummate Our Country's Professional Sports Disciplines Procedures*, J. Cap. C. Physical Educ. 3 (2006).

Part III. Doping and Sport

Chapter 1. General Issues

§1. Anti-doping Background in China

137. In the 1990s, China's sports doping problems were obvious.[55] During the World Athletics Championships in 1993 in Germany, it caused a huge criticism that 10,000 meters world record was dramatically renewed and three gold medals were won by young Chinese athletes who were nameless in the international sports arena. Furthermore, Chinese women athletes won twelve gold medals at the 7th FINA World Championships, and it was widely questioned. Subsequently, Chinese sports delegation had achieved extraordinary results during Hiroshima Asian Games. However, one month later after the game, there were seventeen Chinese athletes whose doping test results were positive, and gold medals of eleven athletes out of the seventeen were canceled.[56] These events have caused serious negative impact on China's sports undertakings. In this context and in order to protect the physical and mental health of athletes, maintain fair sport competition and sportsmanship, and to ensure healthy development of China sports, the former State Sports Committee issued *Interim Provisions of Doping Control in Sports* (hereinafter referred as "interim provision") on February 27, 1995, which has clearly stated that the behavior of doping in sports is strictly prohibited, and it will be carefully checked and shall be severely punished.

138. After more thirty years of development, China has achieved remarkable accomplishments in anti-doping works, which is inextricably linked with the "Zero Tolerance" attitude carried out through by former State Sports Committee, current General Administration of Sport, and COC. Nowadays, positive rate of Chinese doping test is 0.2%, which is much lower than international average of 1%. Meanwhile, anti-doping works of China have been highly regarded by the leaders from World Anti-Doping Agency (WADA) and sports organization of other countries, and they have

55. This chapter is a part of the research results of Dr. Jing Xia, associate professor of Jianghan University, China Postdoctoral Science Foundation Project: A study on the Mechanism of International Sports Dispute Resolution-From the Perspective of Doping Hearing (project number: 2013M530853). Social Science Project of State Sport General Administration: The Study on the Hearing System of China's Doping Violations (project number: 2377SS16114).

56. Yuan Shan, *Yuan Weimin and the Sporting Situation* 28–30 (Jiangsu People's Publishing House 2009).

frequently praised that China is a good example of anti-doping in public. In addition, our doping detection technology has remained in international advanced level. China doping detection laboratory has continuously passed laboratory qualification test organized by IOC and WADA for twenty-six years after the first pass of the test organized by IOC in 1989. By carrying out high level of scientific research and international cooperation, our laboratory has remained in international advanced level.

§2. China's Existing Problems in Current Doping Control Works

139. With the continuous strengthening of national anti-doping legislation, China's doping control works have been completely regulated, but there are still many problems in the following areas.

I. Incomplete Hearing System of Doping Violations

140. In 1995, the former State Sports Committee issued *Interim Provisions of Doping Control in Sports*, with which China established the hearing system of doping violations. At the end of 2007, Anti-doping Agency of General Administration of Sport was established. As the development of the hearing system, it made significant sense. *Management Regulation for Anti-Doping* and *General Rule of Doping Control in Sport* (hereinafter referred as *General Rule of Doping Control*) was implemented in January 1, 2015, which marked the integration of China's doping control works and international standard, and the hearing system of doping violation has been gradually finalized. However, China's hearing system of doping violations is still facing the following problems:

2.1.1 The forms of hearing are not flexible enough. In the system, there are only 3 to 7 persons to form an oral hearing system, no written hearing, as well as sole judge proceeding.

2.1.2 Hearing record, hearing summary and hearing conclusion are important documents for doping violations hearing, but the effectiveness between these documents is not clear.

2.1.3 The hearing committee includes the representative of the sports departments, representative of the anti-doping agency, representative of Individual Sport Association, representative of athletes, athletes support staff representatives, and legal experts. Due to the attendance of government sport department, doping violations hearing has a strong administrative color.

2.1.4 Because of the imperfect management of result and untimely disclosure of information, the function of hearing is being weakened.

II. The Organization of Doping Dispute Settlement and Rules for Adjudication Not Established and Introduced

141. In Article 71 of *General Rule of Doping Control in Sport*, it is stated that arbitration can be applied for decision made according to the general rule: " (1)Whether it constitutes a violation of doping decisions; ... (7) Whether to reduce the ban decision ... ." Thus, although the doping violations hearing belongs to the hearing in advance, the dispute caused by the conclusion is a stimulant dispute, and this type of dispute may apply for arbitration. As is stipulated in Article 72, when the decision involved in other events or other parties and related parties are not satisfied, you may apply for the National Institute of Doping Dispute resolution for arbitration. But unfortunately, China's national anti-doping dispute settlement body and arbitration rules have not been set up so far. So, in order to improve the doping violations hearing system and resolve the doping controversy, it is imperative to establish a national anti-doping dispute settlement body and matching rules of arbitration right now. At the same time, doping arbitration will be one step ahead in the field of arbitration, and provide experience and help for building independent sports arbitration too.

III. The Coverage of Doping Control Needing to Be Expanded

142. At present, China's doping control object is only confined to the field of competitive sports athletes and its relative persons or units. But more and more doping problems have appeared in the entrance examination. Although this stimulant will bring endless troubles, the pressures of entrance examination are pushing parents and students to take risks and to use performance-enhancing drugs to pass the physical test and get extra points.

143. So, relevant national departments should expand the scope of doping control from athletes and some related support staffs to other members of the society, in view of more and more serious drug problems in the field of school sports and social sports. Only in this way, the social impact of doping events can be fully curbed.

Chapter 2. Legal Regulation

§1. China's Special Regulations on the Doping Control

144. For a long time, our country has always inherited the sports spirit and purpose, and strictly abided by the commitment to WADA. In 2004, our country had issued *Anti-Doping Regulations* which is more like a programmatic document. These rules have not stipulated hearing and doping dispute settlement procedures. Other provisions are very general and non-operational. On January 1, 2015, World Anti-Doping Code (WADC) (2015) had been formally implemented. In order to keep up with the pace of the world anti-doping, *Management Regulation for Anti-Doping* and *General Rule of Doping Control* had been approved and came into force on the same day by General Administration of Sport. *Management Regulation for Anti-Doping* and *General Rule of Doping Control* and WADC have been in a high degree of consistency, and fully regulated anti-doping work of sports in our country. Wherein, newly increased contents related to the doping violations hearing are as follows: (1) the range of the doping violations; (2) unified and refined the punishment standard and scale for doping violations; (3) established the system of information disclosure related to the hearing; (4) finalized the stimulant dispute solution and proposed to establish national anti-doping dispute settlement body and to unveil related arbitration rules.

§2. The Factors of Doping Control

145. According to General Administration of Sport, the Doping Control involves all steps and processes from the development of inspection plans to settlement of doping violation dispute, including inspection, testing, investigation, therapeutic use exemption (TUE), results management, hearing, punishment, and dispute resolution etc. (*See* Article 3 of the *General Rule of Doping Control*). Thus it can be seen that doping control is a set of processes with laid down rules and anti-doping works by General Administration of Sport.

I. Control Subject: Anti-doping Agency

146. According to the stipulation of Article 3 of the *General Rule for Doping Control*, Anti-Doping Agency is the main body to start or implement of the doping control. China's Anti-Doping Agency has many levels and categories, including "COC", National Paralympic Committee of China ("NPCC"), national and provincial anti-doping agencies, national and provincial sports social groups, sports event organization, other sports social groups and organizations, etc. Above-mentioned organizations respectively carry out the functions of execution and punishment in the doping control system. The government department and the SAD with the legislative power are not in the scope of Anti-doping Agency.

147. Before establishment of China Anti-Doping Agency (CHINADA), there was no such organization which can independently execute the function of anti-doping organization in our country. It was not clear about management and execution, and executive ability was insufficient. After the 2008 Beijing Olympic Games, China's anti-doping management system has been gradually finalized, and the power of legislation, enforcement and punishment has been clearly divided.

In November 2007, CHINADA was formally established. During the eight-year anti-doping practice, function of CHINADA became prominent gradually, and it had played a leading role in the initiation or implementation of anti-doping in our country, as a result of fully performed their duties.[57]

II. Management System

148. Since 1980s, with the change in the national policy and institutional settings, China's anti-doping management system has gradually formed a government-led, independently borne, legally managed, and effectively operated management system which not only conformed to China's national conditions but also integrated with international practice after the four distinct development stage.[58]

Table 5. The Development Course of China's the Doping Control System

	Big Event	*Characteristic*
First stage	June 1987, National Research Institute of Sports Medicine was formally established and began to undertake the doping test and research works. December 1989, CHINADA, as a unit under the sports medicine institute, had passed the doping test of IOC and obtained the approval qualifications, and begun to undertake the domestic doping test.	1. Established the basic policy of Anti-Doping--Three Strict Policy* 2. No related organization to be responsible for anti-doping affairs, sports departments failed to play its management functions. 3. Anti-doping laws and regulations are inadequate.

57. *See Anti Doping Management Measures* tenth.

58. *See* Lv Yiwei, *Evolution of Anti Doping Management System in China*, Chinese Sports Science and Technology 2010-01, p. 57.

Second stage	July 1992, the Anti-Doping Commission of the COC was formally established. The daily work undertaken by the State Commission of Science and Education Division, specifically including research, coordination and organization of anti-doping related work, etc. February 1995, the Anti-Doping Commission set up an Office and Check. Office located in Science and Education Council of Science and Education Department. Check located in National Research Institute of Sports Medicine.	1. It has formed a situation that the national anti-doping works were unified under the leadership of the State Sports Commission and specific anti-doping executions have been carried out by Anti-Doping Commission. 2. The first time, against doping in sport was written into *the Sports Law of the people's Republic of China* and incorporated into the legal category of the state.
Third stage	May 1998, the State Sports General Administration was reorganized by the State Sports Commission. One of the important duties of the organization is to carry out anti-doping works in the whole country, replacing the Anti-Doping Commission of the COC. The specific works were undertaken by the Science and Education Department. January 2004, *Anti-Doping regulations* promulgated by the state council.	1. This clarifies the management responsibility and dominant position of government in the fight against doping. It has formed a situation that the General Administration of Sport is responsible for and organized the anti-doping work in the whole country, and other relevant departments carry out it within the scope of their duties.** 2. There is no organization which can execute its function independently, so that the anti-doping management is insufficient.
Fourth stage	November 2007, CHINADA was founded.*** After the 2008 Beijing Olympic Games, the responsibilities for doping test results management, publicity and education, etc. which had been taken by Science and Education Department have been officially transferred to CHINADA, and CHINADA should fully perform duties of the national-level anti-doping.	1. Independent national Anti-Doping Agency was established. 2. Had solved the problems of decentralized organization, lack of preparation, unclear of management and execution. 3. Had improved the division of power among legislation, law enforcement, and punishment.

* Starting from 1989, China has developed sticks to the principle of "Seriously banning, strictly examining and severely punishing" of doping. Since then, the State Sports General Administration and the Chinese Olympic Committee have formulated more

than thirty relevant provisions. With the doping problem being spread throughout the society, the struggle of anti-doping is not only difficult in sport, but also the strength of the sports industry is far from enough to solve the problem. Practice has proved that this problem of doping and anti-doping is difficult to solve, if there is no government support and participation, to back of the law.

** The Chairman of International Olympic Committee President advocates and launches governments to join the international anti-doping work according to the situation changes in international anti-doping fighting. Along with the coming up of a series of laws and regulations of anti-doping and related supporting normative documents, it indicates the seriousness and stand firm of China government toward to anti-doping work.

*** The CHINADA is directly affiliated to the General Administration of Sport. Main mission of CHINADA: to participate in the research and formulation of development plans and rules, as well as relevant procedures and standard of national anti-doping; to participate in the preparation of anti-doping categories; to organize and carry out doping test and analysis, as well as result management; to organize and conduct investigations and hearings over anti-doping rule violation cases; to conduct doping test for food and drugs; to carry out anti-doping education, training, scientific research, consulting, international exchange and other activities; to supervise the anti-doping work carried out by sport organizations at all levels and of all kinds; and to be responsible for the construction and management of doping test laboratories and to support their independent analytical work in line with related national and international standards; other matters assigned by the General Administration of Sport. *See* the General Administration of Sport website: *Main mission of CHINADA*, URL: http://www.sport.gov.cn/n16/n33193/n33223/n39896/n2338468/2338676.html.

149. In conclusion, the basic framework of China's current anti-doping management system is as follows: under unified leadership of the State Council, General Administration of Sport is responsible for and organize anti-doping works for the whole country,[59] CHINADA is responsible for specified implementation, and other relevant departments provide coordination and cooperation, with national individual sport organization's active participation and execution of duty.[60]

III. Control Object

150. Control object refers to individuals and units that are pointed to in the whole process of doping control.[61] Since the doping control begins in the inspection and investigation, the object of the doping inspection and investigation behavior is the

59. *Anti-Doping regulations* fourth provisions: "the State Council department in charge of sports organized the national Anti-Doping Work." The sports administrative department of the State Council shall be the General Administration of Sport, so the General Administration of Sport shall be responsible for and organize the Anti-Doping work in the whole country.

60. *See* the official website of the Chinese Olympic Committee: *Anti-Doping management policy and practice in China*, URL: http://www.olympic.cn/china/cover/2004-03-10/103943.html.

61. *See* Art. 5 of *General Rules of Doping Control* and Art. 3 of *Anti-Doping Regulations*.

object of control. During the step of inspection, the one who gets inspected is the athlete in or out of competition and is sampled (including domestic and foreign athletes in competitions).[62] In the investigation, the object being investigated is the individual and unit suspected of doping violations. This is not only limited to athletes. Regulated individuals include: athletes, coaches, team leaders, doctors, and other sportsman auxiliary personnel (including related foreigners).[63] The units that are regulated include: social sports groups, athletes' management units, scientific research units, etc.[64]

IV. Scope of Control

151. The scope of doping control involves all the steps and procedures from preparation of inspection schedule to settlement of doping violation dispute, including inspection, testing, investigation, TUE, results management, hearing, punishment and dispute resolution and other aspects.

A. Inspection

152. Inspection is the first link of the doping control. Specific works include: make a doping inspection plan, notify the players who will get inspected, collect and store samples, and transfer the samples to the laboratory.[65] The CHINADA has the power to implement the in and out of competition doping inspection on Athletes.[66]

B. Testing

153. The doping test is carried out in the laboratory of doping control in accordance with the international standards and qualifications. Detection object is the sample of athlete's urine, blood, and other biomaterial for the implementation of doping inspection. Before the positive test results of sample A or sample B are notified to the players, the National Anti-Doping Agency may request the laboratory to carry out further examination to the sample at any time.

In our country, the laboratory under CHINADA is a laboratory who can comply with international standards and qualification, and the laboratory, known as Beijing laboratory in international practices, is the only laboratory approved by WADA in China.

---

62. *See* Art. 18 of *Anti-Doping Management Measures* and Art. 22 of *General Rules of Doping Control*.
63. *See* Art. 18 of *Anti-Doping Regulations*.
64. *See* Art. 19 of *Anti-Doping Regulations*.
65. *See* Anti-Doping Center website, "Doping Inspection Process", electronic document, http://www.chinada.cn/jclc/index.jhtml, accessed August 2015.
66. *See* "General Rules of Doping Control" Art. 22.

C. *Investigation*

154. According to Article 29 of *Doping Control Rules*: "Anti-Doping organizations should investigate the positive results of detection, atypical test results, biological passport positive results and other possible doping violations." In fact, in the reality of Anti-Doping works, investigation includes both on production, trade, use of stimulants, and the reasons for doping violations, the source of the banned substances and methods, the responsibility of relevant personnel and units, etc.[67] The subject of investigation includes: Athletes' Management Unit, National Anti-Doping Agency, relevant provincial Anti-Doping Agency and other Anti-Doping organizations. As for major and complex doping events, the investigation shall be carried out by the Anti-Doping Agencies and related units organized by General Administration of Sports.[68] Athletes and relevant personnel or units shall actively cooperate with the investigation of Anti-Doping.

D. *TUE*

155. TUE means that the athlete shall submit an application in accordance with the *Management Measures of Therapeutic Use Exemption* when he or she, for treatment purpose, needs to use the prohibited substances or methods specified in the list, and then use it after being approved. If athlete needs to use drugs or methods that contain stimulants, and there is no other alternative, he or she needs to apply for TUE. Implementation of TUE is a common practice to ensure the safety of athletes in sports at home and abroad. In January 2009, National Anti-Doping Agency established the TUE Committee, which has undertaken the functions for approving athletes' TUE application.[69] After receiving the atypical results, CHINADA should review to confirm whether there is an exemption for the effective treatment of drug use in the presence of the sample.

E. *Results Management*

156. Results management is a series of management behavior of doping test results by the implementation of National Anti-Doping Agency. Specifically includes: review the positive test results, atypical detection results, atypical biological passport results and biological passport positive result; notice alleged athletes of doping violations and related parties; decide or cancel the temporary suspension.[70]

F. *Hearing*

157. The purpose of hearing is to protect legitimate rights and interests of the athletes and other party thereto, and to have a fair, impartial and timely settlement of

67. *See* Anti-Doping Center website, "Survey Work Introduction," electronic document, http://www.chinada.cn/jclc/index.jhtml, accessed August 2015.
68. *See* Art. 30 of *Management regulation for anti-doping.*
69. *See* Anti-Doping Center website, "Medical Exemption," electronic document, http://www.chinada.cn/jclc/index.jhtml, accessed August 2015.
70. *See* Arts 37–46 of *General rules of doping control.*

the doping violations. Anti-Doping Agency organize the hearings to hear the statement and explanation of the involved person and interested parties, and comments from other hearing participants, and find out the truth. The Anti-Doping Center Hearing Committee, established in 2012, has undertaken the hearing of doping violation and to confirm whether the involved person or/and interested parties violated or not.

G. Punishment

158. As for doping violations, all of individual sports association, the doping test client and CHINADA have the right to carry out punishment.[71] In general, as athletes registration management units, individual sports association is mainly responsible for the penalties for doping violations. But if the alleged parties of doping violations apply for a hearing, and the relevant individual sports association fails to make the decision on punishment within the prescribed period of time, General Administration of Sport will authorize Anti-Doping Agency to deal with it.[72]

H. Dispute Resolution

159. Doping dispute resolution mainly involves three problems. The first is the scope of the dispute. Article 71 of *General Rules of Doping Control* provides the specific scope of eight types of doping disputes that can apply for arbitration.[73] The second is the way of dispute resolution. According to the nature of the doping controversy and the existing legislation, there is no other way (such as "reconciliation", "mediation", "lawsuit" and so on) to settle the doping dispute, but only can settle the dispute by arbitration. The third is the way to solve the dispute. Article 72 of *General Rules of Doping Control* states that international competitions and international athletes can appeal to Court of Arbitration for Sport (CAS) for arbitration, and domestic events and national athletes can appeal to the National Doping Agency. National Doping Agency can have a comprehensive review for the controversial issues. But what needs to be specially noted hereby is that doping dispute settlement organization has not been set up, and the arbitration rules of doping controversy has not been introduced from the beginning of year 2015 as *General Rules of Doping Control* had come into effect.

V. Basis of Control

160. Doping control has two parts: domestic and foreign. Domestic regulatory documents mainly include: *Law of the PRC on Physical Culture and Sports, Anti-Doping Regulations, Rules Hearing (Interim), General Rules of Doping Control, Management regulation for anti-doping, Working Rules of the Hearing Committee of General Administration of Sport of Anti-Doping Center (Working Rules of the Hearing*

71. *See* Art. 30 of *Management regulation for anti-doping.*
72. *See* Art. 30 of *Management regulation for anti-doping.*
73. *See* Art. 71 of *General rules of doping control.*

Committee), etc. The international part mainly includes: *Olympic Charter, International Convention Against Doping in Sport, WADC* and relevant international standards, etc.

VI. Control Targets

161. In order to protect the physical and mental health of athletes, and promote the healthy development of competitive sports, the international community has placed long-term efforts in Anti-Doping works and made fruitful progress. The purpose of World Anti-Doping System and WADC are as follows: (1) protect the basic rights of athletes to participate in sport without doping, so as to improve the health, equity, and equality of athletes in the world; (2) ensure to form a coordinated and effective Anti -Doping system in international and national level in find, containment, and prevention of stimulants use.[74]

162. On the issue of Anti-Doping, China and the international community have a common stance and same interests. China signed the *Copenhagen Declaration* in 2003, and began to implement WADC and seriously fulfilled her responsibilities in the same year. On January 1, 2015, *Management regulation for anti-doping* and its supporting documents *General Rules of Doping Control* was carried out formally which aims to blow the use of doping in sports activities, to protect the physical and mental health of athletes, to maintain fair competition ethics and order in sports by legal procedures and means.

74. *See* WADC https://wada-main-prod.s3.amazonaws.com/resources/files/wada-2015-world-anti-doping-code.pdf.

Part IV. Sport and Commerce

Chapter 1. General Issues

163. "Sports industry" means a series of economic activities led by sports. It is a kind of value-creating industry by using sports itself functions and its radiation effect, and a collection of economic activities to provide social sports products. The money required for the Olympic Games, for example, and the construction of a lot of venues, sports management, and the development of related products, all of such belongs to the category of sports industry. Sporting Industry includes fitness and entertainment, sports advertisements, sport-lottery industry, sports equipment industry, sports broadcasting sales and so on.

164. In 1992, State Physical Culture and Sports Commission explicitly put forward the program of development of sports industry in China at "Zhongshan Conference;" in 1995, State Physical Culture and Sports Commission promulgated the outline of the *Sports Industry Development*, clearly taking the development of sports industry as a major task of sports front during 1995–2010. In March 2010, the document "about speeding up the development of sports industry guidance" issued by the general office of the State Council identified again the government responsibility in the development of sports industry from the national level, and proposed the sports industry as a new growth pole for promoting China's economic development. In October 2014, the State Council issued the *Advisements about speed up the development of sports industry and promotes the sports consumption*, which suggested in 2025, totally more than CNY 5 trillion should be achieved in the sports industry as an important force to promote economic and social sustainable development.

165. On the whole, the sports industry development of our country is on the rise, and the momentum is promising. Especially in recent decades, with the improvement of our country sports status in the world, the consciousness of sports power stimulated the sports consumption having a linear increasing domestic, thereby giving impetus to the development of the domestic sports industry. Its main performances are as follows.

§1. Sports Competition Performance Market Is Increasingly Popular

166. Professional sports event in China prompted the development of sports industry. Professional league has dominated the main sports market in China. The economic benefits include tickets income, naming rights of league, players transfer market relying on the sports competition performance and all kinds of sports intangible assets, etc. Professional football league in China, for example, in 2014 the revenue of Chinese super league reached CNY 400 million, hitting a new record high with the gross income of all Chinese super league clubs arrived at more than 2 billion; besides the attendance of Chinese super league reached an average of more than 18,000 people, and ranked first in Asia and tenth in the world. It is a fairly large number for our professional sports.

§2. Larger Sports Fitness Market

167. Strong sports promote country strong. Along with our country economic growth, the sports fitness entertainment market also accelerated, especially after the issue of a "national fitness program outline" and "sports industry development outline." Sports activities have been carried out across the country, which promote the development of undertakings of physical culture and sports and strengthen the communication of sports culture. The promotion of national bodybuilding makes the sprouting of a batch of sports fitness entertainment facilities in major cities. This guides people to consumption, stimulate the sports market, and greatly promote the development of sports industry.

§3. Sporting Goods Market Is Increasingly Mature

168. Sporting goods market laid the foundation for our country's sports enterprise development. Sporting goods market in China has currently changed from the situation of less quantity, small scale, single product, and poor quality characteristics of consumer groups, by emerging as a batch of large enterprise with abundant funds and good-marketing. At present, our country has become one of the world's largest sports apparel, sports shoes processing base. The added value of 2006–2011 in our country sporting goods industry expanded year by year, the average annual compound growth rate raised by 17.63%. According to China Sporting Goods Federation, in 2013 China's sporting goods industry (sportswear, sports shoes, sports equipment, and related sports products manufacturing and sales) added value reached CNY 208.7 billion, up 7.8% of year-on-year growth. Sporting goods market has become increasingly mature which laid a solid foundation for the development of sports industry in China.

§4. Sports Gambling Market Taking Sports Lottery as Leader Has Just Started

169. In the mid-1980s, some provinces and some cities in our country tried to issue sports lottery, and in 1994, after approved by the state council across the whole country, began to the issue sport lottery. Sports system successively issued lottery for games such as the Asian games, the national games, the East Asian games, the Olympic Games and so on; large-scale comprehensive sports lotteries laid the foundation for the development of sports lottery. Sports lottery industry, as an important component of the sports industry, has developed to certain scale. It mainly focuses on three aspects: the first is the rapid growth of sports lottery's issuance and the increased efficiency of distribution of earnings and capital use; the second is to establish and improve the sports lottery management institutions and sales team; the third is to develop the national sports lottery computer sales system, issuing the football lottery. In 2011, annual sales of sports lottery arrived at 93.7 billion, which also divided into three categories: lotto games lottery, quiz lottery, and billing of sports lottery. But overall, at present sports betting market in our country, in the true sense, is still in its infancy.

170. From the point of view of the industry, the sports industry market is huge, but the development of Chinese sports industry is facing many problems with the challenges and opportunities coexisting. With the rapid development of sports industry, the huge economic benefits brought by the sports has gradually aroused people's attention and a series of legal issues also need to be deeply discussed. The development of sports industry must also follow all kinds of legal system of market economy, for example, the protection of the economic interests of sports organizations. With the continuous improvement of sports professionalization, sports clubs, and sports league, the organizers of contest sports organization in the process of operation, as the economic subject, is bound to pursue a certain economic benefit, of which the various economic activities need to follow regulation or law and at the same time should also be protected by law, such as sports rebroadcast rights, sports logo protection and so on. But because the development of sports law in China has just started, the legal system related to sports industry is not perfect enough, which has become a bottleneck for the development of sports industry, waiting for the solutions.

Chapter 2. Public Regulation

§1. Media and Television Rights

171. It is generally believed that broadcasting rights belong to the sports organizations to propagate sports competition to the public through media such as radio, television, or network and get pay accordingly. According to the medium of the broadcast of events, it can be divided into radio broadcasts rights, television broadcasts rights, and network broadcasts rights; at present Broadcasting Rights of Sports Event, often said, mainly refers to the television broadcast rights. In China there is no law on the nature of sports rights and of ownership of the right at present, except some regulations and the articles of association, such as the one issued in March 2000 "about strengthening the sports TV broadcast management" by the State Administration of Radio Film and Television, which is the first recognition of broadcasting rights. Also in March 2000, General Administration of Sport of China issued "a notice on the management of television broadcasting rights", in accordance with international practice, stating that sports rights belong to sports event organizer. But it is generally believed that the nature of sports broadcasting rights should belong to a type of copyright, so in the "Copyright Law", "Contract Law" and "Criminal Law" one can find the corresponding protecting gist.

I. The Protection of Copyright Law

172. Copyright Law of the People's Republic of China Article 45 provided that: A radio station or television station shall have the right to prohibit the following acts without authorization therefrom:

(1) to rebroadcast its already broadcasted radio or television program;
(2) to fix its broadcast radio or television program on a sound recording or video recording carrier and to reproduce the sound recording or video recording carrier.

The term of protection for the right referred to in the preceding paragraph shall be fifty years and expires on December 31 of the fiftieth year after the radio or television program was first broadcast.

II. The Protection of Contract Law

173. In business, contract is the embodiment of the consensus expressed between trading parties, which is the most common means to balance and protect the interests of all parties. This method is also often used for the protection of sports broadcasting rights, by entering into a rigorous contract between transferor and transferee of broadcasting rights of sports events to specify the rights and obligations of both sides. Not only it can restrict and prevent all kinds of disputes, but in the event of disputes happened, it can also provide strong evidence for court.

III. The Protection of Criminal Law

174. According to Article 217 of *Criminal Law of the People's Republic of China,* whoever, for the purpose of making profits, commits any of the following acts of infringement on copyright shall, if the amount of illegal gains is relatively large, or if there are other serious circumstances, be sentenced to fixed-term imprisonment of not more than three years or criminal detention and shall also, or shall only, be fined; if the amount of illegal gains is huge or if there are other especially serious circumstances, he shall be sentenced to fixed-term imprisonment of not less than three years but not more than seven years and shall also be fined for:

(1) reproducing and distributing a written work, musical work, motion picture, television program or other visual works, computer software or other works without permission of the copyright owner;
(2) publishing a book of which the exclusive right of publication is enjoyed by another person;
(3) reproducing and distributing an audio or video recording produced by another person without permission of the producer;
(4) producing or selling a work of fine art with forged signature of another painter.

§2. Sponsoring

175. Sports sponsorship, of course, depends on the adjustment of law, but the complexity of sports sponsorship decided it cannot be adjusted by a single law, but by the plural legal departments in comprehensive hierarchy. Sports sponsorship laws relate to several legal departments as Administrative Law, Contract Law, Intellectual Property Law and Anti-Unfair Competition Law, etc. It is further aided by the related legal law (e.g., Sports Law, Advertisement Law, and Contract Law), the respective rules and regulations. State physical cultural administrative department, for regulating the sports sponsorship, introduced some rules, such as "social donation (sponsor) to athletes; bonuses, rewards management interim measures to coaches," etc. According to the law aforementioned, therefore, we will discuss the main legal problems about sports sponsorship.

I. The Legal Issue of Sponsoring

176. The chief problem of sports sponsorship is to confirm the legitimacy of the sponsorship. According to Article 42 of *Sports Law of the People's Republic of China:* "The State encourages enterprises, institutions and public organizations to raise funds on their own for the development of undertakings of physical culture and sports and encourages organizations and individuals to donate to and sponsor undertakings of physical culture and sports."

177. This is a basic principle, which means that the law does not prohibit sports sponsorship, but not all sports sponsorship behavior is legal. It still needs to be combined with other law, judging the legitimacy of the sports sponsorship behavior of concrete. When accepting or offering sponsorship, it must be followed:

(1) Sports sponsorship cannot exceed its limits. Sponsor shall not, by virtue of its position, pressure the sponsor or events to affect the process or result of sports, and even damage the fundamental value of the sports -- integrity, authenticity, and competitiveness.
(2) The eligibility of the parties. According to law, the sponsored party must be a sports organization, athletes, sports organizer and sports facilities as well as the administrative department, in addition to the athletes, any natural person shall not be sponsored party. The enterprises allowed to run business by law are generally free to sponsor any sports activities, events or sports organizations. In order to protect the public interest, the legal qualification of sports sponsor has certain restrictions. Among sports sponsorship, the bulk of sponsorship lay on tobacco, alcohol sponsorship next. When tobacco companies take the sponsorship, as the return, tobacco advertising sponsorship must conform to the "advertisement law" and "the regulation of tobacco advertising management interim measures." Our country law prohibited any tobacco advertising in sports sites and gyms and other public places. Even if tobacco advertising is allowed, the advertising must also indicate the "smoking is harmful to health," and must have the approval of the competent department of advertising. The other kinds of tobacco sponsorship, such as name, logo and souvenirs and others are allowed, but should be first submitted to the state sport general administration and the state administration for industry and commerce for examination and approval. Legal restrictions on alcohol advertising are looser; there are no other requirements except hat the contents of advertisements must conform to the hygiene license matters.

II. Sponsorship Contract

178. Sponsorship contract is the manifestation of the law and also the fundamental basis of court cases if disputes happened in the future. The sponsor and the sponsored party shall involve all expectations in sponsorship deal in order to make the terms and conditions stipulated in the contract clear, that is to say, the sponsorship shall be based on the sponsorship contract.

The classification of the sponsorship contract are as follows:

(1) The exclusive sponsorship and several sponsorships. If there is only one sponsor, it means exclusive sponsorship; if there are more than one sponsors, it is several sponsorships. Usually sponsorship is divided into the status of primary and secondary, namely, the major sponsor and the regular sponsor. The exclusive

sponsor shall enjoy the right of exclusive rights and all marketing rights, but also assume all the sponsorship fees. Main sponsor has the major share approved by the public, and also bear the main share of sponsorship. In practice, the exclusive sponsorship is more seen in the sponsorship for athletes, sports organizations and sports venues, but sports events need several sponsors. For example, the Olympics is the world's biggest sports event, costs of which a sponsor cannot bear. According to the Beijing 2008 Olympic Games sponsorship plan, the sponsorship is divided among partners, Olympic sponsors and Olympic suppliers.

(2) The athlete sponsorship contract, sports organizations sponsored and event sponsorship contracts, sports venues sponsorship contract. The athlete sponsorship contract is a contract limited to the sponsorship to an individual athlete. Enterprise, according to the contract, give the athlete sponsorship payment, and athletes allows the enterprise to use their image in business promotion and goods display thus in this way to achieve enterprise target.

(3) Cash sponsorship contract, in-kind sponsorship contract and the service support contract, etc. The enterprise seems to prefer the in-kind sponsorship contract.

It must be pointed out that sports sponsorship is a kind of civil legal relationship in the nature of contract. If the dispute of sports sponsorship happened, it should first apply to the contract which is in the primary status. Lawfully established sponsorship deal, of course, just have legal effectiveness and have the priority to apply. As for false or invalid sponsorship contracts, which in accordance with the law has no legal force, is not applicable. Sponsorship contracts, in order to control the law risk, had better use written form, which terms should not be clashed with the law, and the signatory should be personal or its agent. Second, if the parties did not conclude a contract or those terms are unclear, the relevant provisions of the "contract law" apply.

§3. Merchandising

179. Sports goods (or sports requisites) is the joint name of all the goods used in the process of physical education, sports and physical exercise. Our country, at present, has become the second largest after the US sports consumer market, but our sports industry is still in the early development stage with sporting goods market having great potential. In order to promote the further development of the industry, it needs to standardize the management of the sporting goods market through legislation. The current legal problems in the sports market mainly include the following aspects:

I. The Legal Protection of Sporting Goods Trademark

180. Trademark right means the owner of trademark enjoys the exclusive right of the trademark in accordance with the law. In the process of development of Chinese sports products market has also formed a large number of well-known brand, which are protected by China's relevant laws and regulations.

181. According to Article 57 of *Trademark Law of the People's Republic of China*, any of the following constitutes an infringement of the exclusive right to use a registered trademark:

(1) Using a trademark that is identical with a registered trademark in connection with the same goods without the authorization of the owner of the registered trademark;

(2) Using a trademark that is similar to a registered trademark in connection with the same goods, or that is identical with or similar to a registered trademark in connection with the same or similar goods, without the authorization of the owner of the registered trademark, which may cause public confusion;

(3) Selling goods that violate the exclusive right to use a registered trademark;

(4) Counterfeiting, or making, without authorization, representations of another party's registered trademark, or selling such representations;

(5) Altering another party's registered trademark without authorization and selling goods bearing such an altered trademark;

(6) Help any others to infringe the exclusive right to use its registered trademark with intention to provide convenience for infringing the exclusive right to use its registered trademark;

(7) Otherwise causing prejudice to another party's exclusive right to use its registered trademark.

Trademark in the field of sports mainly focused on sports trademark management, sports product marks, product names, etc. Among these things the legal protection of sports logo problem is particularly important.

182. According to Article 35 of *Law of the People's Republic of China on Physical Culture and Sports*: Symbols such as titles, emblems, flags and mascots of major sports competitions in China, shall be protected in accordance with the relevant regulations of the State. In addition, the sports logo, as a kind of intellectual property, in the *Trademark Law, Copyright Law, Patent Law and the Anti-Unfair Competition Law* have the legal provisions for protection. For example, *Trademark Law* explicitly forbids that anyone to use the same name or similar text, graphics of governments, international organizations' flag and emblem, etc. as a trademark.

183. In 1996, the Regulations on the Administration of Special Signs promulgated by the State Council included text, graphics, and the name of the abbreviations, emblem and mascot logo which is used in the national and international events in the scope of protection. After China's success of Olympic bid, in order to fulfill the promise to the IOC, China actively strengthened the protection of Olympic intellectual property rights. On October 9, 2001, Beijing issued a local rule—"protection regulations Beijing Olympic intellectual property rights," which included the Olympic related special marks, trademarks, patents, works, and other creations in the scope of protection regulations. Again in 2002, the State Council promulgated "the regulations on the protection of the Olympic logo," which is China's first administrative rules and regulations for the protection of Olympic symbol, and the implementation of this regulation played an important role to strengthen the protection of Olympic symbols and guaranteed the successful hosting of the Olympic Games in Beijing in 2008.

184. China has joined international treaties on protection intellectual property, such as Berne Convention for the Protection of Literary and Artistic Works, Paris Convention for the Protection of Industrial Property, Madrid Agreement Concerning the International Registration of Marks, etc. All these international treaties have become the source of law on protecting sports signs of China.

II. The Protection of Consumers' Rights and Interests

185. Sporting goods market depends on the protection of consumer rights and interests, and after decades of development the relevant laws and regulations to protect consumer rights and interests in China moved gradually toward completion although it released relatively late. In December 1984, Chinese Consumer Society was established under the approval of the State Council. After that, the Consumer Associations at all levels have been set up. In September 1987, Chinese Consumers' Society was accepted by the international union of consumer group as a full member. After China's accession to the WTO, the protection of consumer rights and interests in our country had a rapid development. With the development of consumer rights and interests' protection organization and the deepening campaign of the "3.15", consciousness and ability of consumer rights and interests' protection have been growing.

186. According to Articles 7–15 of *The Law of the PRC on the Protection of the Rights and Interests of Consumers,* the consumer enjoys the right of safety, to learn the truth, to choose, to trade fairly and so on. Our country, through the absorption of the relevant experience abroad and the knowledge of China's national conditions, has formed a series of relevant judicial interpretations of consumer rights and interests protection legal system including *The Law of the PRC on the Protection of the Rights and Interests of Consumers*, *Product Quality Standard Law*, *Food Hygiene Law*, *Anti-unfair Competition Law* and other laws and regulations, which protected the consumer rights and interests.

§4. Ownership of Clubs

187. With the reformation of the economic system, competitive sports tend to be professional and market oriented. In the early 1990s, the Chinese football association decided to reform the national football team established professional clubs; other sports such as basketball, volleyball, table tennis followed the same and established professional clubs. Professional sports clubs, as the participants and the parties of sports market, obtain economic benefits and social benefits with business as the means. Professional sports club, is a market subject, whose market management behavior must be adapted to the current national laws.

I. The Concept and Legal Naturc of Sports Clubs

188. Professional sports club is established with non-state-owned assets by individual citizens, enterprises, institutions, and social organizations, with carrying out sports activities as the main content and taking individual citizens as the service object. Most of the current professional sports clubs in China is a limited liability company.

II. Property Analysis of Professional Sports Club

189. In the process from planned economy to market economy, the method to straighten out the club's property right relations is through channels of club management. According to the operation of modern company system, it is the only way to distinguish the responsibility, right, and interest of the main investment bodies.

According to Article 48 of *General Principles of Civil Law*, "an enterprise owned by the whole people, as legal person, shall bear civil liability with the property that the state authorizes it to manage."

190. At the beginning of the sports professional movement, athlete's technology and the names of the sports teams are belonging to the state of intangible assets, which can compensatory transfer and flow according to the provisions of relevant laws. With other social capital involved, the professional sports club established in this way faced more issues of professional sports club's property rights. To define, the property rights of professional sports clubs are mainly concentrated in two aspects: one is the ownership of club's tangible assets, including cash and physical property, and the other is the intangible assets mainly including athletes, coaches, who are taken as capital into the property. The former has nothing more to say because the similar situation exists in the modern company specification. While the latter is a major problem restricting the development of professional sports clubs.

191. There are three kinds of established modes of professional sport clubs in China; they are alliance, stock company, and single proprietorship. There are not entanglements about property right in professional sport club by single proprietorship. Professional sport club by alliance is a kind of club where an investor purchases the club's denomination right, sport team support by technique and appellation, but the investor does not partake in management. Professional sport club by stock company is a kind of club where an investor offers capital as stock, the sport team offers technique and appellation as stock; the two parties mutually manage, and commonly undertake the risk, share profit and loss according to invested ratio. These two modes all have entanglements about property right of club. To settle these problems, the Sport Bureau should perfectly estimate legislation of sport invisible asset and set up professional organ to estimate sport invisible asset.

III. The Legal Problems of Management and Development in Professional Sports Club

192. At present, the market operation of professional sports club involves the naming rights management, ticket management, advertising business of uniform and field, television broadcasting management, commercial game, and fans and sign products and such other variety of ways. But, in sports associations of professional operation, their way is not all the same (in professional basketball club, for example). In the "*Chinese basketball association registered players and registered club basketball team logo marketing management regulation*" issued by the China Basketball Association: the related business practices of all athletes and sports teams registered in the CBA must be approved by the CBA both at home and abroad basketball market. CBA league takes unified management of national television rights, naming rights, mark product award rights, and the advertising power. And the business scope of the various professional basketball clubs only limit to tickets, local TV rights, four pieces of venue advertising, sponsorship and fans association dues, and other income. And the contents of advertisements are also restricted, so in this limited space most of the clubs only run tickets as main managing projects and a few can successfully operate local television rights and field advertising. It largely limits the club's survival and development, and the club must be given more living space through legislation, which can activate the capital flows of professional sports market and promote the rapid development of physical culture and sports industry.

193. The TV broadcast being one of the most effective businesses on professional sports needs professional sports laws and regulations which make it more conducive to its development according to the market changes. Compared to developed professional sports countries in Europe and America, detailed legislation has made regarding the ownership and protection of television broadcast rights. TV broadcasting rights in our country, with the development of sports professionalization and socialization, are increasingly drawing the attention of the professional sports clubs, which not only has brought the huge economic interests for professional sports club, but also promote the club's own image and expand its influence in the public; therefore they exclaim TV has become "lifeblood" to professional sports. However, as China's TV rights ownership is not clear, legislation is still blank in our country, and especially the monopoly on TV is still a big barrier to the development of television broadcasting rights. The competent department of radio and television in China which formulated CCTV must be responsible for negotiation and should purchase the TV broadcasting of domestic game; other television stations cannot directly buy. This provision does not conform to the international practice and market rules, and is also unfavorable to the development of physical culture and TV. Therefore, our country needs to formulate laws and regulations about sports TV broadcast rights as soon as possible to facilitate the development of professional sports clubs in China.

IV. The Legal Questions of Sino-Foreign Joint Professional Sports Club

194. After the professionalization of sports, it can introduce foreign capital in accordance with law and establish sino-foreign joint venture of professional sports clubs. According to Sino-Foreign Joint Venture Enterprise Law, Sino-Foreign Cooperative Joint Venture Law, the Foreign Investment Enterprise Law, and the Company Law, foreign investment approved by the Chinese government can co-host the joint professional sports club with the professional sports clubs in China in accordance with the principle of equality and mutual benefit.

195. According to Article 2 of *The Law of the PRC on Chinese-Foreign Equity Joint Ventures"* The Chinese Government protects, by the legislation in force, the investments of foreign parties, the profits due to them and their other lawful rights and interests in equity joint ventures, pursuant to the agreements, contracts and article of association approved by the Chinese Government." The attracting foreign investment preferential policies provide a great convenience for foreign capital invested in the field of professional sports in China.

Chapter 3. Private Regulation

§1. The System of Sports Industry Standard

196. The value of sports industry is to promote the popularization of sports and improve people's physical quality, which is closely related to people's life. The sports industry in China will fully keep in line with international standards, which means industry standard practice is also inevitable. Standard is the specific performance of one national product technology policy. Standard is the lifeblood of product as well as the foundation for the development of the industry. Standardization is the bridge of international trade and technical cooperation and the important norms for the orderly development of institutional sector, which can well solve the issues of quality, safety, reliability and compatibility, etc. in commodity exchange.

197. The sports industry involves a lot of aspects, and there are many different kinds of enterprises who provide a variety of products and services. Only in terms of sports goods, except the equipment used in training and contest, there are sportswear, sports shoes, sports drinks, food, nutrition, supplements and the supporting facilities in the sports ground. Our country is a big producing country in sporting goods, but lack of standard system and low reference line have become a "bottleneck" restricting the development of sports industry in China. At the same time, the sports venues such as swimming pool, water park, golf courses provided to the public are also increasing, which need the government to set a standard to the sports industry in the form of commodity with the purpose of establishing the order of a fair market operation and safeguard the legitimate rights and interests of consumers. What is more, internationalization and standardization are important to sports industry. Since our country has joined WTO, it is an urgent requirement to keep in line with international standards and enter into the international advanced level through building a system of sports standardization with reference to the basic requirements of the international sports organizations. In accordance with the provisions of the Administrative Permit Law, the State Council has canceled the administrative examination and approval of general sports activities. Sports products and services standardization has become the important content and means for the government to realize the legalization of the sports industry management, standardize sports market and promote sports products market toward healthy and orderly development.

198. According to the regulation of Standardization Law, as the enacting authority and scope of application, sports standards are divided into national standards, industry standards and local standards and enterprise standards. On the basis of the standard, whether mandatory or not, it can be divided into two categories: compulsory standards and voluntary standards.

199. Referring to Chinese standard information network, it can be found that at present there are eighty-nine national sports standard information, including twenty compulsory standards which are mainly about the regulation of high-risk sports, and the rest are recommended physical standards. On October 4, 2003, the National

Standards Committee and the State Sport General Administration jointly issued the "the general requirements for safety of fitness equipment, outdoor fitness equipment" (GB19272-2003), which is China's first safety standards for outdoor fitness equipment.

§2. Sports Product Quality Certification System

200. Product certification is a kind of social activity accompanied by circulation of commodities, and the exchange of product, with the development of market supervision and management, also needs further development. In the process of circulation and exchange, producers have to prove that their products meet certain quality requirements to expand their market and consumers also hope to know if the product's quality they buy is reliable. With the more complicated functions of commodity, consumers are hard to judge with experience. And also, it lacks credibility just rely on self-declaration. In this situation, the quality of goods proved by the third party thrived, which is the inevitable product of commodity economy.

201. In November 2003, our government implemented the certification and accreditation regulations, which has a great influence on our country. With our country joining WTO, many sectors need to be in line with international standards, and the sports industry, as a sunrise industry of high internationalization degree, must walk in the front of row. Especially in such a populous country we live in, the national fitness has become a basic national policy that is vigorously promoted. The quality and safety problems of public fitness equipment are closely related to people's living which will inevitably affect the implementation of the policy. In the process, the establishing and perfecting of product quality certification testing system is an urgent problem waiting to be solved.

202. Sports product quality certification not only provides scientific mechanisms for government to not only supervise sporting goods market and realize the adjustment of the sports industry structure, but also provides opportunity and way for government to reform supervising methods and realize the separated way of certificating and checking, as well as to provide basis to the third party.

203. Product quality authentication system actively promotes sports products manufacturing enterprises to comply with standard. Sports product quality certification is based on product standards. After an enterprise applied for authentication, it means it not only has to implement the relevant standards but it also, in accordance with the relevant provisions of the specified standards and requirements, has to accept the supervision of the certification body. Therefore, the sports product quality certification is an important means to promote enterprises to carry on the product standards.

204. Sports product quality certification is a powerful safeguard for consumers to purchase safe and reliable sports products. The production with quality certification are matched with authentication marks, becoming silent salesman, which shows that the product has passed the certification of the third-party institution's scientific evaluation of reliable quality. Even it has problems with certification logo products, consumers can also protect their rights through the certification body in accordance with the law.

205. At present, a great number of domestic sports enterprises have passed the certification of ISO 9000 series quality system, which also becomes the feasible measures for sports enterprise to face the challenge of "WTO". After ISO 9000, in 1996, our country began to implement the ISO 14000 series of modern environmental management mode, which will improve the work of clearing pollutant, making the work of our country enterprise environmental protection more standardized and keeping the line with the requirements of the international society for environmental protection, and also provide a valid passport for the enterprise to break green barriers of international trade. In this context, Beijing new century sports goods quality certification center (NSCC) set up in December 2003 approved by the National Certification and Accreditation Supervision and Administration Commission and the State General Administration. By the end of 2004, at least 16 companies, 547 kinds of products have been certificated through the certification program of the NSCC technical committee. It is an important step for certification testing of sports product toward the standardized level.

Selected Bibliography

Cao Keqiang. *Summary of Sports Industry*. Shanghai: *Fudan University Press*, 2004.
Dong Xiaolong & Guo Chunling (ed.). *Sports Law.* Beijing: Law Press, 2006.
Gu ShiQuan. *The China Sporting*. Beijing: Beijing Sport University Press 2002, 2006.
Gao Mingxuan & Ma Kechange (ed.). *Criminal Law*. Beijing: Peking University Press, Higher Education Press, 2007.
Guo Shuli. *The Plural Remedy Mechanism of Sports Disputes, Comparative and International Law Perspective.* Beijing: Law Press, 2004.
Han Yong (ed.). *Sport and Law – View on Sport Dissension Case.* Beijing: People Sport Press, 2006.
Huang Jin, Xu Qianquan & Song Lianbin. *Arbitration Law*. Beijing: China University of Political Science and Law press, 1999.
Jiang Renbing & Liu JuChang. *The Sport Law*. Heilongjiang People's Press, 1994.
Liu Depei & Bai Junling. *The Sports Reform in China for 20 Years*. Beijing: People's education press, 2001.
Li Changqi (ed.). *Economic Law.* Beijing: Law Press, 2008.
Liu Juke. *Sports Law*. Guilin: Guangxi Normal University Press, 2005.
Ma Junju & Yu Yanman. *The Theory of Civil Law.* Beijing: Law Press, 2005.
Ma Kechang (ed.). *Theory of Crime*. Wuhan: Wuhan University Press, 2005.
Ma Huaide. *The Law and Procedure of Administrative*. Beijing: China Legal Publishing House, 2007.
Song Jianying. *The New Theory of Sport Administrative Law*. China University of Political Science and Law Press, 2010.
The Writing Group of Sports History Materials. *Sports History*. Academic Publishing, 1996.
Tang Weidong. *Sports Law*. Nanjing: Nanjing Normal University Press, 2000.
29th Olympic Games Organizing Committee. *Assembly File of Olympic Intellectual Property.* Beijing: Law Press, 2005.
Wang Quansheng. 'Research on Legislative Efficiency – with Contemporary China as the Legislative Perspective'. Beijing: China Legal Publishing House, 2003.
Wu Handong (ed.). *Intellectual Property Law.* Beijing: Beijing University Press, 2005.
Yang Liming & Yu Yu. *Contract of Sports Event.* Beijing: Law Press, 2007.
Yu Yulin (ed.). *Modern Invisible Asset.* Beijing: Economic Science Press, 2007.
Zhang Houfu. *Sport Jurisprudence*. Beijing: People's sports press, 2001.

Selected Bibliography

Index

The numbers here refer to paragraph numbers.

Index

Index

Made in the USA
Monee, IL
18 October 2026

66037582R10077